Hope and the Approaching Apocalypse
Sustained by Prophecy and Science

William Clark

Parson's Porch Books

Hope and the Approaching Apocalypse
ISBN: Softcover 978-1537511016
Copyright © 2016 by William Clark

All rights reserved. No part of this book may be reproduced or transmitted in any form or by any means, electronic or mechanical, including photocopying, recording, or by any information storage and retrieval system, without permission in writing from the publisher.

To order additional copies of this book, contact:

Parson's Porch Books
1-423-475-7308
www.parsonsporch.com

Parson's Porch Books is an imprint of Parson's Porch & Company (PP&C) in Cleveland, Tennessee. PP&C is an innovative company which raises money by publishing books of noted authors, representing all genres. All donations from contributors and profits from publishing are shared with the poor.

Hope and the Approaching Apocalypse

Contents

Foreword		9
Introduction		11
Chapter 1	"True Science"	13
Chapter 2	"The Elements of Truth"	18
Chapter 3	"The Coming Apocalypse"	25
Chapter 4	"Beans, Guns and Water"	38
Chapter 5	"The Glory Has Departed"	46
Chapter 6	"UFOs and Lost Files"	59
Chapter 7	"The Six Millenniums"	67
Chapter 8	"The One Less Traveled By	86
Chapter 9	"Adam, Eve and Advanced Biology"	102
Chapter 10	"The Good, the Bad and the Prophets"	118
Chapter 11	"The Laws of God and Science"	134
Chapter 12	"He Is Coming Real Soon"	150

Dedicated to my family

And to those who seek the truth

Foreword

Dr. Roger Ewing

Hope and the Approaching Apocalypse is a book that certainly gets one's attention. William Clark does much more than presenting an apocalyptic belief based on prophecy and science. He weaves the state of the world and society with the facts of prophecy and science to demonstrate a true connection with the upcoming apocalypse.

Over seven years ago, I met Bill Clark where he was the pastor of a local church in Indiana. I was part of the music program, and even though Bill was the pastor, he also helped with the music. He is a Biblical preacher, which is indicative in the book. Bill and I became friends, and we also talked about many situations over lunch and coffee.

We are advised not to read the end of a book first. It's like watching only the end of a movie. After reading each intriguing chapter, Bill emphatically gives a power punch at the end of the book. The churched and the unchurched will appreciate the message that we should all be prepared. In every chapter you can feel the concern that the author has for the state of the world and for our personal well-being.

If you like to read or listen to the news, you won't want to put down the urgent messages in "The Approaching Apocalypse".

Introduction

Do faith and science prove or indicate that there is something to all of the attention surrounding the apocalyptic clamor? I'm sure that many of us are wondering why so many people are obsessed with the apocalypse. We not only see cable documentaries and movies about the apocalypse, but we also hear about it at church and through other associations. By now, everyone has heard about preppers; even FEMA is preparing in a big way. Is it a fade or is there something to it?

The obsession seems to be with not just one group or religion, but it includes a variety of people and ages. About four years ago, I was shopping at a large chain discount store. A young man in his twenties started talking to me about prepping. It seemed that his belief in the coming apocalypse had to do more with being prepared for a nationwide or worldwide catastrophe. He was preparing with several other young people and an older man, who owned a shelter in the country. They were gathering food, water, medical supplies and weapons among other things. One cable documentary interviewed a young, prepper woman, who concentrated on physical fitness and a "bug-out" system in a big city, because she felt civil chaos would take place due to a global oil shortage. I would think that a dedicated prepper wouldn't be living in a big city!

Believers in the soon coming apocalypse also seem to be from diverse educational and financial backgrounds. A good example of diversity is my own brother, Dr. Richard Clark, who has his own practice and is affiliated with a prestigious medical school. It might be of no surprise that an evangelical like myself would tend to believe in the apocalyptic age, but some may be surprised that many like my brother also believe in the approaching apocalypse.

When our mother's health declined, my brother and I met a number of times in our hometown. Our lives had taken different paths since graduation from high school and college. My older brother pursued a career in medicine; obtaining several specialties and an undergraduate degree from M.I.T. After college, my life took me into evangelical ministry. I traveled from Indiana to Texas, and later became a pastor and retired as a pastor.

As we caught up with each other, we were both surprised to learn that both of us believed that we are living in the apocalyptic age. We see faith and science merging together, as we experience the closing of the current era of mankind. I first began to get a sense of this by the end of my undergraduate days. My brother began to sense it much later from his scientific and mathematical knowledge. He has studied a number of theories, and believes that based on science and mathematics, the apocalyptic age is upon us.

Perhaps there is more to the Hollywood movies and television documentaries on the apocalypse than just money and ratings. There seems to be a desperation in our times that not only looks to religion for answers, but to preparedness due to the fear of world-wide catastrophes ranging from pandemics to nuclear warfare to natural disasters to food and water shortages. Religious believers, preppers and even scientists are unwittingly merging together in the belief of the apocalypse.

In a number of apocalyptic documentaries today, we here the phrase, "it's not a question of if it will happen, but when it will happen". Increased knowledge will take us from apocalyptic fanatics to realists as we explore science, religion, personal convictions and the unstable world in which we live.

Chapter One

True Science

As science evolves, does it confirm the accuracy of the Bible? Do science and faith complement each other? Your answer might depend upon the ranking order you give to three words based on the criteria of truth: God, the Bible and science. If you rank science first then God or the Bible, you might find this chapter thought provoking. If you ranked God first then the Bible and science, then you probably realize that without the omnipotence and omniscience of God, there is no scientific or Biblical truth for mankind. It's interesting that God's infinite knowledge is described as "Omni-Science" (omniscience)!

To paraphrase the Bible's claim to truth from God, it says that prophets of old did not write words from themselves but holy words that were given to them by inspiration through the spirit of God (the Holy Spirit). (2 Peter 1:21 NIV) May I appeal to your logic by giving some examples? The prophet Isaiah around 700 B.C. wrote in Isaiah 40:22 that the earth is round, "He sits enthroned above the circle of the earth, and its people are like grasshoppers. He stretches out the heavens like canopy, and spreads them out like a tent to live in" Also, Job 26:10 refers to the earth being round.

Almost every humble and arrogant scientist and everyone else from before 700 B.C. to almost 1500 A.D. thought the earth was flat! The Bible could have given those early scientists a big leap into the future. Does that thought apply to scientists today? Let's look at a couple of other Biblical examples. Another verse in Job 26, verse 7, also shows that the Bible taught what science didn't learn until over two millenniums later; that the earth floats (described later as revolving) in space, "He spread out the northern skies, over empty space; he suspends the earth over nothing". Whereas, Hindus were taught in the past that the earth was supported on the backs of four tremendous elephants that stood on a huge tortoise, which floated on the surface of the world's waters. Today we can confirm the Bible's teachings in the books of Isaiah and Job that the earth is suspended over nothing by images we receive from satellites.

The Bible also taught in the Old Testament book of Leviticus that life is in the blood; over 2,500 years before the medical profession reversed its practices of bloodletting. Leviticus 17:11 in the New International Version (NIV) says, "For the life of a creature is in its blood". The New Living Translation says, "For the life of the body is in its blood". (The King James Version is very similar.) Also, in Leviticus 17:14 we find, "the life of every creature is its blood".

"The practice of bloodletting began around 3,000 years ago with the Egyptians, then continued with the Greeks, Romans, Arabs and Asians". (BC Medical Journal Vol. 52, No. 1) Of course, it was also practiced in Europe and America. (We'll look at this practice again in 1799 America.) Dr. Hughes Bennet (1812-1875) was one of the doctors who helped set the stage for the removal of bloodletting as a standard practice. Unfortunately, bloodletting was still practiced in the 1800s.

It's easy to see that bloodletting as a whole was an erroneous and harmful practice that was conducted for 2,800 years. It makes us wonder about certain practices today that are harmful to our health and environment. Based on facts, we could propose the hypothesis: The Bible is an open page to truth for science. We'll look at other examples, which show that science and faith complement each other.

I've been a proponent of natural, nutritional products since the early 1980s. I've wondered for many years why chemotherapy is so widely practiced and accepted. "Three doctors of four would refuse any chemotherapy themselves". (Albert Braverman, M.D. "Medical Oncology in the 90s" Lancel, 1991.) In 2014, it was again reported that most doctors would not use chemotherapy as a treatment for themselves. Like hazards of bloodletting, chemotherapy can adversely affect different parts of the body. Many people know from experience that research as well as second and third opinions from doctors should be considered. I know of a drug that adversely affected my mother and a pharmacist friend. The pharmacist could have used an alternative drug, but at that time, he didn't realize that the drug would put his healthy body in a wheel chair. Why was bloodletting practiced for about 2,800 years, and why are chemotherapy and certain dangerous drugs being prescribed today? Some physicians and scientists (including a talented biochemist, who I know) feel that questionable practices exist because of economic and social interaction. There is no doubt that the dynamics of teaching and career politics also enter the picture.

    I conducted a funeral service several years ago, and had dinner with some of the family members. One of the sons told me that about thirty years ago his first cousin came to a family gathering one weekend and was real excited, because his research firm in Ohio discovered a cure for cancer. When he went back to work on Monday, one of the company officials told him to hand over the paper work that he had on the new cancer drug. When he asked why, the company official bluntly said that the file is being closed on the new drug and that nothing is to be said. The family member's first cousin was so disappointed and disillusioned with the company that he left employment with them.

    Our country is use to cover ups. "Fast and Furious" (the debacle of the guns from the federal government sold to criminals) began between September and October of 2009. On

September 28, 2011, Forbes said, "September 2009 is the earliest we can trace the operation". Forbes reported, "ATF field agents soon began to question the sanity of letting guns "walk". We wonder today what happened to the sanity of our government and society.

Reports finally came out between 2013 and 2016 from the federal government and CIA that Area 51 does exist. (If you're interested, it's in Nevada's Mojave Desert.) You can get good information about Area 51 and UFO files from two of my favorite channels: The History Channel and History H2. Area 51 had been a government secret since 1955. Cover-ups also exist about our environment, but many scientists and environmentalists are working hard to improve our environment.

The Bible and science have been two of the most honest entities for millenniums. Isaac Newton was a mathematical genius. Isaac Newton was born on Christmas of 1642. He actually invented calculus. (He invented the mathematical theory that became known later as calculus.) He also invented the reflecting telescope and developed the theory of gravity and the laws of motion. Newton was also a gifted student of the Bible. He said, "This most beautiful system of the sun, planets, and comets could only proceed from the counsel and dominion of an intelligent and powerful Being".

Newton believed that science proved God's supreme rule. Newton said, "Since every particle of space is always and every indivisible moment of durations everywhere certainly the Maker and Lord of all things cannot be never and nowhere. God is the God, always and everywhere". Newton's truth and greatness can be read in his classic work, "Mathematical Principles of Natural Philosophy".

Joseph Lister is known as the father of modern surgery, and he was also a Christian and student of the Bible. Lister was born in 1827. His family were Quakers, and he graduated from the University of London in 1847. Lister wrote, "I am a believer in the fundamental doctrine of Christianity".

One could say that modern science roots are in the Bible today, and in the days of Kepler and Mendel, and in the beginning of Biblical records. Kepler believed that mathematics and astronomy reveal God to others. He was a great mathematician and astronomer. Among his accomplishments, Kepler proposed that the moon causes the ocean tides to ebb and flow. He was also the first to explain planetary motions.

Mendel is known as the father of genetics. He also headed a monastery in Austria. In Mendel's time, people knew him as the abbot of his monastery rather than as a great geneticist. People admired him as a Christian, but they didn't know about his scientific genius. Mendel developed the laws of inheritance and discovered the inter-workings of dominant and recessive genes.

Some of the greatest scientists from our time and from the past 400 years witness to faith and science complementing each other. Sometimes we think of the reformation founders like Luther, Knox, Calvin and Wesley as the modern cornerstones of faith. It is also significant to see Newton, Kepler and Mendel as cornerstones of faith and science. More and more doctors and nurses are telling us that prayer is an important process in healing. We don't hear it a lot today, but more and more scientists and doctors are seeing how faith and science merge together.

Chapter Two

The Elements of Truth

Pilate asked Jesus, "what is truth?' Christ knew that Pilate wouldn't accept his answer, so he remained silent. Christ's disciples though were receptive to his answer. Long before his trial, Jesus explained to his followers, "I am the way, the truth and the life". (John 14:6 NIV) When we have a national debate with presidential candidates, how many of them and their constituents would agree that Christ's definition of truth is the answer to the nation's problem? I doubt if we will hear that during the 2016 presidential campaign or during any other national campaign. Many people today are unwilling to stand for the truth.

Most older colleges and universities that were founded by Christian denominations have been ransacked by humanistic teaching. I grew up in a society where the news media did truthful and impartial investigative reporting. Now the humanist media is so biased politically that the public gets propaganda instead of true news and political reports.

In several thorough surveys in the last five years, 60 to 70 percent of high school students admit to cheating on tests, and 95 to 98 percent admit to cheating in school on assignments and on copying homework. The conservative publication, Reader's Digest, took a poll way back in 2004 about telling the truth. At that time, 93 per cent of the people polled admitted to being dishonest at work or at school. 96 per cent admitted to lying or being dishonest with those close to them. Imagine today the rampant dishonesty within social circles and at work.

Today television runs many unorthodox reality shows. Two of them though portray the traditional ethics of putting God first: Duck Dynasty and Dog, the Bounty Hunter. Their uniqueness puts their faith in the fore front. In Duck Dynasty, they are shown taking a stand for what is right. In Dog, the Bounty Hunter, they are shown praying and encouraging fugitives to tell the truth. If our society would once again teach their children the ten commandments and to tell the truth, our traditional values would once again surface to make America strong in substance and in morality.

Most every avenue of society is crowded with habitual liars. It's not just in politics and at work, but it is also found in the field of science. Evolutionists have lied to themselves and to the public so much that they are convinced that evolution (outside the species) is a fact and not a theory. Let's agree that Darwin be the judge by looking at his comments. Darwin and most people have no problem in seeing and understanding evolution within a species. In a tropical climate, we can see how birds have adapted with longer tail feathers and more color. In a colder climate, it's easy to tell from the lineage of man that many people have lighter colored hair. But what does Darwin have to say about specific examples of evolution outside the species. Does he really believe that man came from monkeys and that reptiles came from insects?

Most evolutionists have convinced themselves without empirical evidence that there has been evolution from one specie to another. They believe reptiles have become birds and that the animal kingdom evolved from cells like amoebas.

I like the story of the young boy, who went to his father and asked him if we come from apes; the father said, "yes". He then went to his mother, and asked her if we come from apes, and his mother said, "no". The little boy replied, "but daddy said that we come from apes". His mother said, "that's his side of the family". There is no evidence of evolution from specie to specie. The Bible gives much more evidence of species being created of their own kind and reproducing their own kind. But let's get back to what Darwin said.

Lingering doubts troubled Darwin concerning evolution from one kind of specie to another. He was troubled so much that he edited his, "Origin of Species", from one edition to the next. (Darwin's Doubts by Stephen C. Meyer) Evolution presentations are at best conjectures or theories. They are suggestions from imaginations similar to the suggestive powers of Spider Man and Thor. Darwin commented on the human eye as an example, "The eye to this day gives me a cold shudder". Darwin said that to think the eye had evolved by natural selection is "absurd in the highest possible degree".

The evolutionary evidence that we have occurs within a specie. Unfortunately, much of the public and evolutionists have come to believe their lies. What is occurring today in evolution instruction can be aptly explained by Darwin: he said, "imagination must fill up the very wide blanks". Some archeologists would like new fossils to "fill the gaps" between the old and the new, but what fills the gaps is the archeologist's creative imagination.

Even in the field of ministry, for over forty years I have experienced deception at times, whether I was working as a full-time evangelist, associate or pastor. There are counterfeits for everything: saline solution or sugar water for a promising medicine; fake doctor of divinity degrees; a new, natural vitamin that will give you the energy of youth that you had 30 to 40 years ago; a "trusting" attorney; an anti-Christ and even counterfeit for the dollar bill!

I doubt if Pilate was sincerely looking for the truth, when he asked Jesus that question. But fortunately, many people are looking for truth in science, education, church, employment and other fields. Our search must start with an open mind and an honest heart. Even if the earth is one of the oldest planets, are we really living in the apocalyptic era? Can we find wisdom and truth in fields like science, education and religion?

Every scientific field from archaeology to astronomy has found abundant information that is helpful to mankind, but each of us has to decipher the truthful information. We must weigh the information, like we would weigh and decipher information from the internet and from news media. Truth should be the constant goal.

Albert Einstein said, "Science without religion is lame; religion without science is blind". For roughly eighty years, about 40% of scientists said that they believe in God as the creator. Dr. Craig Rusbult aptly states in his paper on scripture and nature what this author has shared, "God has graciously provided us with two sources of information: in the Bible and in nature". Dr. Rusbult goes on to quote a very timely verse from Psalm 19, "the heavens declare the glory of God".

Does science merge with faith in time? We should ask ourselves if science brings us to greater faith, and conversely, if faith brings us to a better understanding of science? If our answer is "yes" to both, then it's wise to look at many issues in the world, like evolution and the apocalypse, through the eyes of faith and science.

Before we look at the apocalypse from a scientific view, let's briefly look at one more popular subject in the world of evolution, the age of the dinosaurs! A lot of us have already heard about the critical inaccuracies in carbon 14 dating. Another problem with dating dinosaurs is the gross differences in results from dating methods. A potassium argon method may date a dinosaur bone at 5 million years while a carbon dating method may date the same bone at 150 million years. One can't get much more inaccurate than that. A number of institutions have thrown out results, when the results didn't support the imaginary age of the researchers' resolve.

Carbon 14 dating only has some accuracy for a few thousand years. On the other hand, even then it can be inaccurate. A carbon 14 test was done on living penguins, and the results showed that the penguins were 8,000 years old!

The problem is not with science, but it is with those evolution researchers and teachers who want to believe that dinosaurs lived on earth millions of years ago!

In the May 31, 1990, issue of The New York Times, it was reported that "scientists have long recognized that carbon dating is subject to error, because of a variety of factors, including contamination by outside sources of carbon". In other words, carbon dating is inaccurate not just from one problem, but from a number of problems.

Facts about dinosaurs not being millions of years old have been censored form some geological societies. A paleo chronology group reported their finding of eight dinosaurs found in Montana, Colorado, Texas and Alaska (using carbon 14 dating) in 2012, They found after taking multiple samples of bone from all eight dinosaurs that they were from 22,000 to 39,000 years old.

I understand that two groups would probably not believe these findings: strict creationists and evolutionists. It's ironic that some creationists would say that the bones aren't that old and most evolutionists would say that they're not nearly old enough! I realize that this is not a book of philosophy, but let me, for a few words, propose some logic.

The Bible does say that to God, one day is like a thousand years and that a thousand years is like one day. (2 Peter 3:8)) The Old Testament book of Job in Job 40:15-24 speaks of the "behemoth", "Look now at the behemoth, which I made along with you; he eats grass like an ox. ...He moves his tail like a cedar ... his ribs like bars of iron". Before I retired as a pastor, I listened to an interesting prophecy teacher lay out three different proposals about the state of Israel and the United States in the end time. The teacher was well informed, but he didn't pressure his students into believing that he knew the precise prophetic state of America or Israel at the end time. He left to his students, the task of deciphering the information and deciding for themselves. Whether one is a creationist, an evolutionist or somewhere in between, they also have to decipher the information and decide for themselves. The Apostle Paul said that mankind has to work out their own salvation; meaning that we are responsible for deciding what we think is right. Possibly the evolutionists are wrong, and the creationists could be partially wrong. Maybe the dating of the 22,000 to 39,000-year-old dinosaurs was off. Maybe if we knew the truth, the dinosaurs were really 6,000 to 7,000 years old! Like the timing for the return of Christ, only the Father in heaven knows the hour.

Truth is the gauge for true science and true faith. Most evolutionists are not true scientists, because of their inaccurate dating methods and their wild exaggerations. Albert Einstein was correct by pointing out that science and religion are only true and more virtuous, when they are partnered. True science and true faith confirm the value of each other. There are two worlds pointing to end time events: the worlds of faith and science. In several chapters, we'll look at additional specifics.

As I write these words today, Billy Graham turned 97 (November 7). He claims that the apocalypse and the return of Christ are "near". Benjamin Netanyahu has announced that "biblical prophecies are being realized", and other political leaders like Michele Bachmann of Minnesota believe that the world is in its last days. The Christian, Jewish and Muslim faiths all believe that the Messiah will return at Armageddon (the Valley of Jezreel – see chapter 3 and chapter 12). Are scientists as adamant about the end of the age as followers of faith?

Atomic scientists have been setting the dial on the "Doomsday Clock" for 68 years. It's not encouraging to know that they have moved the minute hand recently to three minutes to midnight. The board for The Bulletin of Atomic Scientists, who control the doomsday clock, have had 18 Nobel Prize Winners as members, and they have moved the hands of the clock 18 times in the past 68 years. They analyze the world's technology, environmental and political changes and activities. They could move the hand back, but facts like Russia and the United States having 26,000 nuclear weapons keep the hand moving forward.

Obviously, atomic scientists use different logic than people of faith, but it's a fact that the world renowned atomic scientists also believe that we're very close to the apocalyptic age. Are other types of scientists also studying the proximity of the apocalypse? The answer is an indefatigably, yes!

One of the newer institutes studying the end time is the Future of Life Institute at M.I.T. Another United States' Institute is the Machine Intelligence Research Institute in Berkley, California. One of the leading global institutes on the apocalypse is the Future of Humanity Institute at Oxford University. They were founded in 2005, and have a team of mathematicians, economists, computer scientists, physicists, biologist and philosophers studying the apocalypse. Chapter 3 will cover some of the subjects that they're studying. In 2012, a similar institute opened at Cambridge University, the Centre for the Study of Existential Risk.

Chapter Three
The Coming Apocalypse

To get a better understanding of the coming apocalypse from a scientific view, let's look at the apocalyptic risk information from institutes like the Future of Humanity Institute at Oxford. Some scientists break down the list of risks into twelve categories, and some scientists break down those categories. A list of twelve apocalyptic risks are 1) Nuclear War 2) Global Pandemic 3) Super- volcano Eruption 4) Earthquake and/ or Tsunami 5) An Asteroid or Meteor Impact 6) Extreme Climate Change (food and/ or water shortage) 7) Nanotechnology 8) Artificial Intelligence 9) Ecological Collapse 10) Unknown Consequences 11) Global System Collapse (including civil and economic break down) and 12) Synthetic Biology (engineered pathogen and/or chemical warfare).

The highest risk factors of 10% each were given by scientists to Super Intelligence and Unknown Consequences. Many researchers, including myself, think there is a greater risk from food and water shortages, nuclear fallout, natural disasters and from a global pandemic (like Europe and Asia experienced during the Bubonic Plague). Besides the possibility of an asteroid or meteor impact, there are other atmospheric conditions that could be apocalyptic: a solar flare storm, gamma ray burst, black hole, toxins in the air, ground and water and others. In the 19th and 20th centuries there were solar storms that caused widespread damage to telegraph and other communications. Some scientists say that the earth dodged a bullet from a large solar storm in July of 2012.

We don't know how close the world has been to someone pushing the nuclear button, or to a terrorist obtaining a nuclear weapon. Some scientists also look at the relativity of extinction caused by a catastrophic event. Extinction is not two to four billion deaths, but it's the annihilation of the entire human population. The possibilities of different apocalyptic events mirror prophecies and merge with what prophets have said for over 2,000 years.

Even though chapter six will partially cover the debate between alien invasion and divine intervention, the world has documented many reports of divine intervention, but alien invasion is mostly speculation. Much of the world, including Christians, Jews and Muslims, believe that the apocalypse will be ushered in by the hand of God. Most of my life, I've heard some people say that every generation says the Lord is coming back soon. Some say that the world has always had earthquakes, hurricanes, tsunamis and other natural disasters. I understand why people make both comments, but is there something special about the current age? Are we very close to the end of the world as man has known it for several millenniums?

Before we look at prophecy, we'll look at what scientists say, then other professionals and finally prophets. Apocalyptic critics say that the world has always had natural disasters. CRED is the Center for Research on Epidemiology of Disasters (in Brussels, Belgium). CRED and the OFDA, Office of U.S. Foreign Disaster Assistance, report that natural disasters have been steadily increasing in recent decades: from 78 in 1970 to 348 in 2004. In 1980, there were about 100 disasters, including droughts, tsunamis, hurricanes, typhoons and floods, but after the year 2000, there were about 300 per year.

Disasters that worry scientists in the U.S. are: heat waves, the largest disaster killer in United States history, which also took my grandfather; fault lines, the cause of earthquakes and tsunamis; Midwest fault line, the site of America's greatest earthquake, almost 200 years ago. The fault line is near New Madrid, Missouri. The fault line is now heavily populated. Heavy population in the New Madrid area includes St. Louis, Ferguson, Columbia and Memphis. Scientists say that the New Madrid earthquake will be felt from South Carolina to Massachusetts. They also say that some homes along the Mississippi would sink into oblivion". (live science, August 23, 2010.)

Also, the super-volcano at Yellowstone would cause half of the country to be buried in as much as three inches of ash. A Los Angeles Tsunami also worry scientists. It is also a possibility that a meteor will hit again. A hurricane could also hit New York City. It takes a 24 hour notice to evacuate NYC, and scientists say the warning may only be a few hours. Scientists say that a San Andreas earthquake would be deadly, but the ensuing tsunami would be deadlier. Many experts say that we are not adequately prepared for a nationwide catastrophe, and that we should be preparing now.

Scientists warn us of coming catastrophes. Does God? God does many times through his prophets, and through his son, Jesus Christ (who the Muslims call a prophet). In Matthew 24, Jesus said the signs of the end would be as in the days of Noah. But there is even more to what Jesus said, then what we find in the Matthew passage. The Matthew passage gives reference to people eating and drinking and marrying before the flood in verse 38, which shows that people will be living typical lives before the apocalypse. But if we refer to the story of Noah in Genesis, we find why mankind grieved God. God "saw how great man's wickedness on the earth had become, and that every inclination of the thoughts of his heart was only evil all the time". (Genesis 6:5-NIV) The next verse says that God's heart was filled with pain. God was so grieved that He had made man that He said, "I will wipe mankind, who I have created, from the face of the earth". But verse 8 says, "But Noah found favor in the eyes of the Lord".

The flood was the first great apocalyptic event; so much so that God almost wiped out mankind. It's astute to remember that other civilizations like the Hindus, South American tribes and Native American tribes recorded the event of a great flood. Genesis says that God promised Noah and mankind the rainbow as a sign that mankind would not be annihilated. Many years ago I stopped along coastal highway A1A, south of Ponte Vedra, Florida. There was a beautiful, full rainbow that reached over the ocean, and I just had to stop the car to take in the beauty. There was a young couple standing nearby, and I said, "it's a beautiful site". They replied that they loved looking at the rainbow. I asked them if they knew that the rainbow is God's Covenant with man. They said they hadn't heard. I shared the covenant of the rainbow account with them from Genesis 9. Even though mankind has this great promise from God, the apocalypse will still come before things get better. There have been times in history when it must have felt like the apocalypse and the day of the Lord were coming. No doubt the Black Plague, the American Civil War, WWI and WWII with the atomic bomb blast in Hiroshima and Nagasaki must have felt like the world was coming to an end during those times.

At the time of the atomic bomb detonations over Japan, only the United States had completed the development of the atom bomb. Unfortunately, many countries have the atomic bomb now, and some are not allies of the United States. Whether by science or by prophecies, it is speculation on how the apocalyptic events will unfold, but by prophecies we have a good picture of what will happen.

The words "Armageddon" and the "apocalypse" are used loosely today. They have been prophesied by old and new testament prophets and by Christ as well as by prophets like

Nostradamus and Edgar Cayce. "Apocalypse" refers to catastrophic end time events that led up to the final apocalyptic event, which takes place in Israel. Before things get better, the final event is not "Armageddon", but it takes place in Armageddon. Armageddon is one of several names for the large valley of Jezreel, which is in Israel, an hour and half north of Jerusalem and northeast of Tel Aviv. The town of Nazareth borders the Valley of Jezreel on its north side. Armageddon (the Valley of Jezreel) has also been called the Valley of Megiddo, which contained the ancient city of Megiddo. Many armies have fought there, including the Crusaders, the Romans, the Turks, the Greeks, as well as Gideon and Israelite armies. The prophet Joel refers to it as the valley of decision. (Joel 3:13-14 NIV) "Armageddon" is found in the Bible in Revelation 16:16. The name of the end time event is "the great day of God Almighty". (Revelation 16:14) It's the great battle of God and his people against the armies of the world.

Most anyone would be curious about the situation and the events of the world that prelude this great battle. There are actually a large number of prophesies that tell us what happens before the great day of God Almighty. Jesus told us that many would come in his name to deceive us. He also said we would hear of wars and rumors of wars. He said that nation will rise against nation. He said there will be famines and earthquakes in various places. He said that his followers would be persecuted and put to death. He said that many false prophets will appear and deceive many people. He also said that many would leave the faith and betray his followers. (Matthew 24:4 - 28 NIV)

Today it seems that there are so many national conflicts, that sometimes nations ally with the enemy of their enemies. America has been in conflict with Russia for many years and more recently when they invaded the Ukraine. Now with Russia bombing in Syria, we become an ally, because we're both fighting Isis. It's hard to figure if we're an ally or enemy of China, because of all the cyber-attacks against the United States. Today we could be an ally of China, and tomorrow we could be in cyber warfare with China. Sometimes we don't know if we're a friend or foe of Turkey. We're supposed to be an ally, but yet men fly from Turkey to Syria and to Iraq to fight with Isis.

Jesus also said that "many would also come in my name". Some religions don't recognize Jesus as the Messiah or as the Son of God. Other religions take bits and pieces of the Old and New Testament, then create their own text or Bible. Revelation 22:18 -19 says, "If anyone adds anything to them (the words and prophesies of this book). God will add to him the plagues described in this book. And if anyone takes words away from this book of prophecy, God will take away from him his share in the tree of lie and in the hoy city, which are described in this book".

Jesus said that his followers would be persecuted and put to death. Christians have been put to death in Rome, China, France (French Huguenots), England (William Tyndale, King Charles 1 and many others), Nazi Germany, Russia and many other countries. Today some Muslim countries imprison Christians or put them to death. Christians are also being put in prison and being executed in other countries. There is a greater persecution of Christian in the United State. The newer trend of humanism has influenced the radical left to persecute Christians. A once, open-minded news media in America has morphed into a main-stream media that is politically bias and usually opposed to traditional, Christian values.

Jesus also said there would be famines and earthquakes in various places. Famine is one of the apocalyptic disasters along with water shortages. In 2015, 3.5 million children died from starvation. 300 million children go hungry every day. One in 8 to 9 people don't have enough food to have a healthy life.

Two thirds of the people in Asia are hungry. In parts of Africa, one person in four is undernourished. Hunger kills more people each year than AIDS, malaria and tuberculosis combined. (Mercy Corps)

Jesus specifically mentioned earthquakes, that with ensuing tsunamis could wipe out a large portion of the earth's population. Scientists list the New Madrid fault line and the San Andreas fault line as two of the most potentially, deadly areas in the United States. Earthquakes along with generated tsunamis could be one of the greatest apocalyptic catastrophes.

The 2004 Indian Ocean earthquake and tsunami killed 280,000 people; the second worse tsunami in history. The second deadliest earthquake in history was the Tangshan earthquake in 1976; roughly 650,000 people were killed. In just 2010, the Haiti earthquake killed about 200,000 and injured over 300,000. In 2003 the Kashmir earthquake killed 100,000, and the Sichuan earthquake killed 88,000 people. The 1976 Tangshan earthquake and the 2004 Indian Ocean Tsunami were the second and eighth worst natural disasters in history. These statistics are taken from records of the larger natural disasters that have been recorded with their death toll for almost 2,000 years. In 115 AD an earthquake and tsunami devastated Antioch, when it was in the Roman Empire. Another earthquake in the 6th century killed about 250,000 people in Syria, when it was under the Byzantine Empire.

It doesn't take a PhD. to see how natural disaster prophecies are being fulfilled, as the disasters increase in frequency with time. CRED experts in medicine, psychology, geography, economic, sociology, nutritional sciences, and public health have found that natural disasters have been increasing during the recent decades. Fortunately, OFDA experts respond to an average of seventy disasters per year in fifty-six countries.

Samaritan's Purse responds to victims of war, natural disasters, disease, famine, poverty and persecution in over 100 countries. For seventy years, UMCOR has been aiding global victims of floods, earthquakes droughts, war and other disasters. UMCOR also assisted a lot with the Katrina Hurricane relief and the Haiti Earthquake relief. Other great organizations assist with disaster relief, but there may not be nearly enough help for the events of the apocalypse.

Another eerie situation during the apocalyptic disasters is based on a belief of many evangelical Christians. Many relief organizations are sponsored by Christian churches and groups, like Samaritan's Purse and UMCOR. There are other Christians and a lot of seminary instructors who also believe that they won't be here when the apocalyptic disasters take place. (We'll look at the basis of those beliefs in the last few chapters.) If they are right, the Christians who work and volunteer for those organizations, will not be here, and the world will not have most of the disaster relief that they have now.

Even though Christians, Jews and Muslims believe that God or the Messiah is returning to the area of Jerusalem, the event that they believe in is at the end of the apocalyptic disasters, instead of at the beginning of the apocalyptic era that leads to "the great day of God Almighty". It's interesting that many persuasions of people believe in the apocalypse, but there is not an expansive or consistent apocalypse belief between the many professions, classes and religions of people. Christians and non-Christians alike express a desire to learn more about Revelation, but some of the most simple and clear passages concerning the apocalypse are not pointed out to them.

In the Bible, the last book of the New Testament, Revelation (which was written during the early days of the church around 90 AD), is not as complicated as many think, if the book is laid out in sections. The Apostle John, one of the original twelve disciples of Jesus, opens the book by saying that Revelation is the revelation of Jesus Christ, which God gave him. The revelation was delivered by an angel to John, so the Apostle John could receive God's Word and testimony of Jesus Christ. (Revelation 1:2). It is also very noteworthy to consider verse three, where a blessing of God is given. God blesses those who 1) read the words of the prophecy, 2) hear it and 3) take it to heart. The verse concludes by saying, "the time is near".

Chapters one through three in Revelation are about seven early churches; chapter four describes God's glory; chapter five addresses the authority and power of Christ; chapters six and seven are the introduction to the events of the apocalypse or tribulation; chapters eight through eighteen are about the apocalyptic or tribulation events and crises, and chapters nineteen through twenty-two are about the great day of God Almighty; God's deliverance and new home for his people. Even though prophets like Nostradamus and Edgar Cayce predict some events during the time of the apocalypse, no prophecy is so thorough as Revelation concerning the apocalypse and the finale at Armageddon.

There are some other prophecies in the Bible that are as pointed as those in Revelation about events leading up to the apocalypse and to the great battle at Armageddon. One of those prophecies was told by Jesus as found in Matthew 24, Mark 13 and Luke 12: "Now learn this lesson from the fig tree. As soon as its twigs get tender and its leaves come out, you know that summer is near". (Matthew 24:32 NIV) The Old and New Testaments contain God's description of Israel as a "fig tree" (by the prophets). It is widely accepted by Bible scholars that Christ in these passages is referring to Israel. Even though Israel seemed to have no prospects of regaining its land after Roman armies destroyed Jerusalem shortly after

70 AD, they did. About 1,918 years after the prophecy of Christ, the powers to be, after England, the United States, and Russia won victory over Germany and its allies, enabled Jews to return to their homeland.

Of course Palestinians protested as well as some other Muslim countries, but they were not the world powers that were victors over Nazi Germany. Of course, today not only are the Palestinians actively protesting the Jewish presence in Jerusalem and Israel, but so are Iran, some other Muslim countries, and Muslim radicals who want to do Israel harm. Iranian leaders and followers, Isis, Al- Qaeda and others, threaten to "wipe Israel off the face of the map". Israel is more gracious to them, because Israel is the one in the conflict that possesses nuclear weapons.

I wonder if leaders of Iran, Isis and Al-Qaeda lie awake at night, since Israel could wipe them off the face of the earth. Liking or not liking Israel or the Old or New Testaments of the Bible is like a true story of a survey that was taken in church. The church leaders wanted to know what the congregation's favorite hymn is and their least favorite hymn. When they calculated the results of the survey, half of the congregation chose "In the Garden" as their favorite hymn, and half of the congregation chose "In the Garden" as their least favorite hymn. As well as Christ's prophecy about Israel, the Old Testament also has prophecies about Israel returning as a nation.

Revelation answers some very specific questions about the apocalypse. Revelation 3:10 answers how sincere people can avoid the apocalypse: "Since you kept my command to endure patiently, I will also keep you from the hour of trial that is going to come upon the whole world to test those who live on the earth". In a future chapter, we'll look more at the people who can avoid the apocalypse, including the time of the battle at Armageddon. Significant individuals like Christ and the

Apostle Paul also explain how these particular people will avoid the apocalyptic, end time events.

Is it just prophecies like those of Jesus that foretell the disasters like earthquakes, wars and famine that are coming to earth with greater intensity? A news report today (November 21, 2015) reminded me of the intensity that is coming soon. The night before, (November 20), many residents in Kentucky, Ohio and Indiana saw an unusually large comet falling in the sky. It was caught on camera and reported like a passage from Revelation. In chapters 7, 8 and 9 of Revelation as well as several later chapters, we find passages about locust plagues, earthquakes, tsunamis, wars, famine and meteors (asteroids) falling.

Many preppers and believers of the apocalypse today speculate about the events and finality of the end times (as we know it). Revelation again paints by far, the clearest picture of the final events of the apocalypse, including the final battle of good against evil. Some scholars refer to these events as the great tribulation, which basically means the end of the end times. Besides Biblical references from Christ, Paul, Jeremiah, Daniel, Ezekiel, Joel and references from Nostradamus and Cayce, the Apostle John gives us the most vivid account of the end of the end time in various passages of Revelation. In chapter 17:14 of Revelation (NIV), the inspired author describes the apocalyptic foes as well as the victor: "They (God's enemies) will make war against the Lamb, but the Lamb (Jesus Christ) will overcome them because he is Lord of lords and King of kings- and with him will be his called, chosen and faithful followers".

There are two scriptures, one from the Old Testament and one from the New Testament that not only complement each other, but they also complement the research done by scientists and Nobel Prize Winners with The Bulletin of Atomic Scientists; Albert Einstein; Isaac Newton; scientists and other researchers with the Future of Humanity Institute; scientists and other professionals with the Centre for Study of Existential Risk, the Center for Research on Epidemiology of Disasters, and the Office of U.S. Foreign Disaster Assistance. Revelation 6:17 is a very significant chapter that ties together Old Testament Prophecies (Isaiah 13:6-10 and Joel 2:28-32) and some New Testament prophecies, including Matthew 24:29, with current scientific research and predictions. The apocalyptic scripture (Rev. 6:17) says, "For the great day of their wrath has come, and who can stand?" Two verses earlier, the passage describes everyone on earth, from the great to the common; being terrified by the events of the apocalypse.

Isaiah is one of several respected (in his day and ours) prophets to describe what Revelation describes as well as modern scientists, "The stars of heaven and their constellations will not show their light. The rising sun will be darkened and the moon will not give its light. I will punish the world for its evil, the wicked for their sins. I will put an end to the arrogance of the haughty and will humble the pride of the ruthless". (Isaiah 13:10 NIV) These are the words God gave to Isaiah as his anointed prophet. Even though a non-believer of God's word may doubt the validity of this passage, it is not hard for even an atheist to understand what modern scientists and other researchers are warning us about.

As I was writing this chapter, I coincidentally saw the movie, "San Andreas", with the Rock (which is an interesting name since Christ is referred to as "the Rock"). In the opening of the movie, a professor of geology is instructing his class on earthquakes, including "the big one". In the scene he makes the statement, "it is not a question of if it will happen, but when it will happen". Even though linguists today would call this a trite statement, because it's so widely used, but in reality it is not trite, because of the impact of its truth. When I was a kid, a popular comedian performed a skit about another apocalyptic event, Noah and the flood". The comedian's famous question is uncannily provocative in our era, "how long can you tread water"?

Chapter Four
Beans, Guns and Water

My wife sometimes wonders about my stockpile of canned tuna and pork and beans, but within a month it diminishes, when I donate to the local food pantry. I also give to a homeless mission. Giving is a good reminder of what it's all about; helping those created in the image of God. Giving is a wonderful, godly principle. Wisdom is another godly attribute, and I would share with anyone that it's wise to have an emergency supply of food and water. If you have read the Genesis account of Joseph in Egypt, then you know about the rise of Joseph to second in command of Egypt. During time of plenty, pharaoh gave Joseph the responsibility to see that all of Egypt stored food to be used during the time of famine. The Bible in Matthew and Revelation prophesies that famine will be one of the disasters during the apocalypse. Everyone should be encouraged to store food and water for times of need.

On December 11, 2015, USA Today ran a weekend, cover page article entitled, "Our Water Is Running Out". (by James and Steve Reilly with "The Desert Sun") The U.S. Geological Survey has found that in the past two decades, ground water levels have decreased in almost two-thirds of the country's wells. The research covered 32,000 wells. Many of them are in eight states from South Dakota to Texas. This area has been one of the world's most productive farming economies.

The area is known as the High Plains Aquifer or "The Ogallala", which produces much of the country's wheat, corn and cattle. The USGS (U.S. Geological Survey) has found that more and more wells are going dry. It's not just the eight states of the High Plains Aquifer. There are also ground water levels plummeting in areas of California, the Gulf Coastal Plains, farmlands in the Mississippi River Valley and in the Southwest and parts of the Southeast. Other problem areas are along the Atlantic coast. There have also been long term declines in Milwaukee, Chicago, Houston and Memphis. Parts of Mississippi, Arkansas, Missouri and Louisiana are using much more than what's being replenished.

USGS scientist Leonard Konikow said, "Like your bank account, you can't keep depleting it forever; that's a non-sustainable condition". (contributing reporters, Steve Elfers of USA Today and Caitlin McGlade of the Arizona Republic) Joseph, Egypt's second in command over 3,500 years ago, had Egypt save six years for times of famine. He realized that when the reserve drops, there is less to count on in times of need. The USGS has discovered the same need with our nation's water reserve. In the southern High Plains, water levels have plunged more than 100 feet in 20 years. Drilling has been going deeper at great costs.

It's alarming that the USGS has found that water levels have declined in 64% of the wells in the last two decades. While many wells are going dry across the country, residents in California's Central Valley get water delivered to them by tanker trucks. NASA satellites have found widespread ground water declines from North Africa to India. Jay Famiglietti, a professor of earth system science at the University of California Irvine and NASA scientist said, "We never really, understood it the way we understand it now. It's pervasive, and it's happening at a rapid clip". Problems with ground water also hurts the economy and inflames ownership disputes.

Christ's prophecy of famine in "the last days" will obviously be impacted by current and future shortages of water. When there are shortages of food and water and serious economic problems, countries and individuals that were once peaceful can turn to civil unrest. Preparation seems to be a key at this time.

After briefly looking at concerns of food and water shortages, are guns and ammo the next concern? Guns are an individual choice, but I will make some common sense comments. First of all, when guns are illegal, criminals and our other enemies are the only ones who will have them. Secondly, if Isis or any other enemy infiltrates our society, the public will wish that the government had left the NRA, National Rifle Association, alone. About twenty-five years ago, I had a business acquaintance, who called me one day at work. I asked him how he was doing. He said that he was miraculously recovering in the hospital. He said that he went to an ATM machine outside a bank, and a man came up and shot him three times. Learning that experience from a friend, acquaintance or report would motivate almost anyone to get a gun carrying permit. If people let the government keep you from having a gun and a permit, there will be more murders and even less protection in our volatile society. The author is not saying to go out today and buy a gun, but if your local gun shop, Bass Pro Shops, Dick's Sporting Goods, Gander Mountain or anyone else still sells guns and ammo, you might want to do some shopping.

It's more than just a coincidence that more and more people are preparing for catastrophes from the natural to the man-made to financial. The National Geographic polled 1,000 people, and found that 61% believe there will be a catastrophic event in the near future. Why such a dismal forecast? Is there really something to it? Some reports claim that several million people in the United States are preparing for the apocalypse. One report says there are three million people who are preparing (preppers). They didn't include me in their survey, so there are at least three million and one people prepping for catastrophic events. I believe a lot more are prepping and stockpiling food and water, as well as medical supplies.

One of the best websites that help people prepare is "survivalblog.com". James Rawles, who served as an US Army intelligence officer, set up the very informative website and help guide. His survival website is updated daily. The content of the site assists people in several ways. It gives item and contact information for different survival needs. People also contribute articles from gardening to investing. It has an archives that goes back over ten years, so the prepper or the curious can do extensive research for their needs. There is also an index that gives references to their glossary of terms; how to use the site and link to other sites. The website also has an alphabetical index of categories from aquaculture to field gear to survival mindset to weather.

There's a wide range of preppers. Some basically stock food, water, and warm clothing and coverings like blankets and sleeping bags. I like to include light sources to the basics, which include candles, matches, flashlights, and batteries. Some preppers have backup systems: generators, tents, extra gas and other resources. More extreme preppers go to great lengths from building and stocking bunkers and fortresses. One family built a fortress on a hill with a number of defenses in their fort, as well as on the hill leading up to the fort. A man filled his swimming pool with 1,000 fish so he would have plenty to eat during dire straits, and one family built an underground bunker and stockpiled weapons with 25,000 rounds of ammo.

Once again, stockpiling for emergencies is helpful physically as well as psychologically. Being prepared physically is not a full proof preventative, but it does give the person or family assurance that they will be taken care of; at least temporarily. The family that built the fortress on the hill may be able to keep their fortress from one or two strays trying to steal from them, but if ten or twenty people storm the hill, the fortress will be passed on to the greater force. The man with the 1,000 fish in his pool won't survive from the fish, if the water becomes contaminated during a catastrophe. The family with the underground bunker and weapons is limited to the severity of the disaster or to the number of people who overtake the bunker. The main factor is who we put our trust in. Even though the nation does not practice our national motto, "In God We Trust", people can observe it as individuals, families and communities.

    Most people should not need much evidence that "the big one" is coming, because many people, churches and businesses are talking about it. Bill O'Reilly of Fox News has referred to it as "the big train". FEMA, the Federal Emergency Management Agency, is stockpiling food, blankets, trailers, tents, medical supplies and body bags. The Department of Homeland Security is buying huge supplies of weapons, ammo and riot gear.

    The following quote is from MyPatriotSupplies.com: "Here we are, and FEMA once again is trying to buy up large stockpiles of food. And they don't want anyone to know it... that is what got me into preparedness in the first place". (Before It's News – February 4, 2015) The author has heard similar things from his own professional sources.

    The frequency of TV commercials and internet reports by celebrities like Ron Paul and William Devaine, warning us about the dollar and the astuteness of buying gold or silver would make me sit up and notice, if I wasn't in agreement already. Ron Paul is a talented physician and politician whose advice shouldn't be taken lightly. Many preppers also believe that an economic crisis is coming soon. Is the shaky, global economy one of the indicators of the approaching apocalypse?

    It makes me take notice, when leading economists say that the looming economy will make the 1929 depression look like a church picnic. Many economists and some political leaders are now admitting that the dollar will be replaced as the world currency standard. One reputable economist said that when the dollar is eliminated as the world's currency, the 2008 crash will look miniscule in comparison.

The leading economists who predict the upcoming crash say that the United States will have large and widespread inflation. They predict that there will be large increases in the costs of essential commodities like food, gas, clothing and more. They also say that the country will have much more difficulty financing the national debt. They predict that there will be much higher interest rates on mortgages, big ticket items and credit cards. Some economists refer to the crash as the collapse of the U.S. dollar.

As of November 27, 2015, the national debt is over 18.7 trillion dollars. The debt crisis is clarified more by looking at the national gross, annual income, and the annual interest paid on the debt. The total U.S. federal revenue for 2015 is estimated to be 3.25 trillion. In 2014 almost 431 billion dollars were paid in interest on the national debt. Back in 2011, Representative Randy said, "Each day our nation pays communist China $73.9 million in interest on our debt". Forbes also said that our interest payments to China allow them to "aggressively modernize their military and increase their global influence". Our country's spending in 2015 will be about 3.7 trillion dollars. It's scary to think that federal income for 2015 will be about 3.25 trillion dollars; that's an annual deficit of .45 trillion dollars, which is the same as 450 billion dollars. One might conclude that our national debt is increasing about .5 trillion a year, but that is far from the truth. Our government is spending more money and paying more interest than we realize. Almost every year since 2008, the national debt has increased by more than 1 trillion dollars per year. If Obama stays in office until the end of 2016, it is conservatively estimated that the country's debt will be more than $20 trillion dollars.

Currently the national debt has increased about 70 percent under the Obama administration. When Obama took office the national debt was 10.6 trillion. As of November 27, 2015, the national debt is 18.7 trillion. Obama has created more debt than Reagan, Bush Sr. and Clinton put together, and Obama has created almost twice as much debt as George W. Bush. By the time Obama leaves office, he will have put the United States in as much debt as all of the other presidents together.

The problems don't end with the national debt and the Obama administration. China wants a new global currency to replace the dollar. Arab states have had secret meetings with China, Russia, Japan, Brazil and France about replacing the dollar with a new world currency. It's predicted that China will become the number one economy in 2016. Even the World Bank has admitted to the decline of American economic power. With China's financial power leading the way, India is also interested in the change of world currency (the two largest, national populations in the world).

Let's stop and look at a few quick facts. America was strong when the country's faith in God was strong. At one time, with little interference by organizations like the ACLU, America truly trusted in God. We were Bible centered, but now the nation has moved far left of center. Our country has evolved into a socialist government with a socialistic party recently leading the way. A student of the Bible knows that when Israel trusted in God and followed God that they were blessed. When they forsook the ways of God and worshipped other gods and robbed God of tithes and offerings, they were cursed. America's spiritual problem today is that the country doesn't honor God.

Jesus Christ said there would be wars and rumors of wars in the last days. It also looks like an economic war and civil struggle is coming to America. Some analysts predict that the loss of the U.S. dollar would quadruple the cost of living, and lead to riots and great civil unrest. At the conclusion of this chapter, you might be feeling that you live on the bottom floor of a two story outhouse, but the light is still there.

In the gospel of Mark in chapter 13, we'll told three different times to watch and be prepared. The disciple also tells us to be on guard and to be alert. Being prepared means to be prepared more than just physically and emotionally, it also means to be prepared spiritually. In the Old Testament, the prophet tells us that people without a vision perish. We need to know who to trust in; we need to know where our faith is. People who pray and have faith in God will be prepared much more than extreme preppers.

Chapter Five

The Glory Has Departed

Philosophers, historians and theologians could agonize over the purpose of the United States and its greatness. Is it like Rome? Rome had slavery, so did America. Rome as an invader was usually cruel to the inhabitants of the land; so was America to its Native Americans. Yet Rome also had its silver lining; so does America. Rome had Constantine, who made Christianity the state religion. The United States was largely developed by people who had been persecuted for their Christian faith. Rome conquered countries, where they usually allowed the people to keep their religion and culture; so has America.

The 64,000-dollar question is: does God still have a purpose for America (the United States)? Today the left wing radicals think they are the current purpose for America. They are rhetorical hypocrites and delusional. They claim to be sensitive to the causes of people and to be politically correct; and by the way, what is politically correct? George Washington, Abraham Lincoln, Andrew Jackson, Teddy Roosevelt, Franklin D. Roosevelt and Ronald Reagan were politically correct, and the left wing radicals aren't anything like them!

Our country is facing increased terrorism and more threats of terrorism in the face of 9/11. California, which has strict gun control laws, was just terrorized in San Bernardino be two radical Muslims, who killed fourteen people and injured seventeen (December 3, 2015). We should always remember that if we let them take our guns away, only the terrorists and other criminals will have guns and bombs. The French have some of the strictest gun controls in the world, yet terrorists in November, 2015, killed over one hundred people in Paris.

The left wing radicals in this country think they are "politically correct", when it serves their purpose. If a Christian or a conservative speaks out, and the left disagrees, then all of a sudden the radical left turns from Dr. Jekyll into Mr. Hyde! Are they schizophrenic? Maybe not psychologically, but they certainly are politically and socially.

The Daily News ("New York's Hometown Newspaper") blasted Christians and conservatives on December 3, 2015, for requesting prayer for the victims and families of the San Bernardino shooting. The Daily News said, "God Isn't Fixing This", on their cover story. They quoted and criticized Ted Cruz, Dr. Rand Paul, Lindsey Graham, Paul Ryan, and others for requesting prayer. The Daily News called requesting prayer, "meaningless platitudes".

Welcome to the radical left in America! It started with radical leftist instructors brainwashing young college students in the last fifty plus years. It has spilled over to the mainstream media and their socialist beliefs. Now the mainstream media admits their bias. The mainstream media with their bias reporting brainwashed the American public into voting the last two presidential elections for the current administration in Washington. The Daily News, Gene Weingarten and their left wing comrades are trying to shame the public into gun controlling instead of praying. When I was a kid, an Indianapolis TV channel after the 11:00 PM News would ask, "Do you know where your child is?" Today we should ask, "Do you know if your child has been brainwashed today?"

Does the radical left in America play into God's hand today? If we look at America's culture today, America's political left, the Bible and science, we will find a common denominator. The United States like many countries is facing terrorism from the Islamic, Isis terrorists. Just recently Isis has expanded from parts of Syria and Iraq to northern Libya. The United States has a current president (2015 and 2016), who thinks that climate change is a more urgent problem than terrorism! Actually climate change is way down the list after terrorism; Isis; the economy; global economy and political strife; 60 million babies in America being killed by legalized abortion; the down fall of American infrastructure; and the lack of faith in America's (the United States') culture today, rather than a nation that trusts in God. We're hearing every day about how little the radical left trusts in God.

True science also puts the squeeze on the radical left. Leading scientists, as well as science for generations, disputes the radical belief that climate change is the world's worse problem. The increased problems with a potential nuclear disaster; world-wide pandemic; super-intelligence; spatial problems including asteroids and solar flares; increased natural disasters; drought; famine; humanism; greed; wickedness and terrorism do not fall behind climate change as the world's worse problems. Jesus Christ and other spiritual prophets and secular prophets predicted ages ago that these are the problems in the last days. A fumbling and blundering radical left cannot stop the direction the country and world is taking. Only faith and God can change the course.

How many times have we heard the saying, "what goes around, comes around"? Does America and her citizens feel that we're exempt from the ancient, Biblical saying, "a man reaps what he sows"? Some would say that from slavery in America, the country reaped a whirlwind. During the American Civil War 620,000 soldiers from the north and the south lost their lives. In school text books we read about the civil war, but we didn't read about the Dawes Act in public school text books and how the act affected the lives of our Native Americans.

A few tribes in the East weren't affected by the act, but most tribes were west of Wisconsin, including Wisconsin, Minnesota, North and South Dakota, Montana, Kansas,

Nebraska, Oklahoma and other states were greatly affected. The act was passed by Congress and signed by Grover Cleveland, because the public was told that it was created to assimilate the American Indian into our culture. The results of the act were horrific. The act broke up tribal sovereignty, and attempted to assimilate the individual Native American family to their own, small farms. The Dawes Act accomplished reducing Native American land from 150 million acres in 1887 to 60 million acres in 1930 (by selling Indian land to settlers).

Even though the Dawes Act was revoked in 1934 by President Franklin Roosevelt's signature, problems continued for Native Americans. We also weren't taught in school that Catholic and Protestant boarding houses and schools were established for Native American children. Several years ago I visited a Native American reservation in South Dakota. I met a missionary and local Native American people helping their people at the reservation. I also met with one of the tribal council members, who told me about atrocities that happened to his own family. He said until about 1970, the local boarding house and school for native children were still in operation. He shared how officials from the boarding school would come to the homes of their tribe, and take their children away, when they turned five years old.

The tribal council member told me that the children were not allowed to speak or pray in their native language. He said that both his mother and grandmother were beaten and raped as children by officials at the boarding school. He also shared what I have also heard from other sources. He said that many reservations in the United States have landfills, prisons and dams built on or next to the reservations. Of course, this practice further diminishes Native American land and their health.

Suicide, alcoholism, drug addiction and widespread poverty continue to be devastating problems on Native

American reservations. Some courageous Native Americans have dedicated themselves to following the ways of Jesus Christ and peace. Some of the Native Americans from the Dakotas make a 328-mile horseback ride from South Dakota to Mankato, Minnesota, every December to commemorate 39 Dakotans who were hung in December of 1862 by the federal government. It was the largest execution in American history. Like Dr. Martin Luther King, these Native Americans invoke peace and forgiveness by participating in the annual horse ride. It's noteworthy to mention that the well-known United Methodist minister and author, E. Stanley Jones, studied peace taught by Christ and by Gandhi. Martin Luther King use to share that he learned a lot about peace from the writings of E. Stanley Jones.

Martin Luther King did not forget about slavery in America, but he forgave the country as well as those who practiced bigotry. Many Americans today don't practice peace and forgiveness, regardless of their race. Many church people are taught about love, peace and forgiveness, but most aren't taught about the judgements of God.

Even the types of teaching and preaching have changed in many American churches in the last forty years. Unfortunately, they too have succumbed to "theological and political correctness". People are glad to hear about God's love, but they don't want to hear about God's judgments (in theology today, this practice is called the "social gospel").

Most church people are taught that followers of Christ are saved by grace; not by works. Unfortunately, they are not taught two significant scriptures: Romans 2:6 and Revelation 20:13. The New International Version (may be even more accurate than the King James version based on the original Hebrew, Aramaic and Greek texts) in Romans 2:6 says, "God will repay each person according to what they have done". The

NIV in Revelation 20:13 says, "and each person was judged according to what they had done".

The individual must decide if America was in "God's grace" during the Great Awakening years. The first Great Awakening (a religious or Christian revival period) occurred in the 1730s and 1740s. The second Great Awakening was from 1790 to when it reached its peak in 1850. During this time, both Baptist and Methodist churches experienced tremendous growth. Some historians claim that a third Great Awakening occurred between the late 1850s and the early 1900s.

During the early 1900s, the Methodist church revoked John Wesley's requirement of a weekly fellowship meeting (prayer and Bible study) as a continual requirement for church membership. After the weekly requirement was revoked, Methodist membership began to fall off. Secular and theological historians call the 19th century the "Methodist Century". Many Methodists and other people today do not know from their churches or history classes that in the 19th century, the Methodist church was known as "the camp meeting or revival church". It is possible that their evangelical spirit began to gradually wane after the early 1900s. (The Pentecostal movement came out of the Methodist church in 1909.)

Philosophers or laymen could speculate that America has lost its spiritual guidance by God. Of course, the atheist's answer is obvious, but traditional Americans have the knowledge that America was once a nation that trusted in God. Now much of the population trusts in the propaganda of the mainstream, socialist media and spiritual apathy of publications like "The Daily News".

The generation of World War II knew what it was to trust in God. I was raised by parents from that generation. Sadly, most of the Great Depression and World War II generation have passed on. (I lost my father ten years ago and my mother one year ago.) My concern is about the generations since that time. Many of the baby boomers are still in church, but many of my children's generation and those between them and the millennials are not in church.

At the same time, America currently has a president and administration that seem to undermine the country. They have shrunk our military while Isis, Iran, China and Russia grow stronger. When our country defeated Germany and Japan, our soldiers and other aid workers stayed there to help protect the countries. Not so with the current administration, after Saddam Hussein was defeated under the previous administration, our troops stayed in Iraq to help protect and support them, but the current president doesn't understand how to protect. He didn't listen to the wisdom of his best military advisors, and he made a very costly decision by pulling American troops out of Iraq. He had no military experience, but the country put him in charge of the military. We can't put the blame of Isis on one person, but he would probably come closest to the blame.

We do have historical facts from the Bible of how Israel prospered under God's direction, and suffered after his departure. There are many examples of this phenomena in the Bible, but some of the clearest and most dramatic examples of how Israel was blessed with God and cursed without God are found in the Old Testament book of Ezekiel as well as in the book of Judges.

Before looking at these Biblical accounts, the author proposes a hypothesis. Science does not base its findings on "correctness" (except for evolutionists). True science bases its findings on the facts of results from accurate experiments and proven studies. Even though today's politics and society are based on "political correctness", true science does not bend to "scientific correctness". In an upcoming chapter, we'll look at authentic studies of history and archeology concerning Biblical accounts. The author's hypothesis is: Biblical accounts can assume to be accurate based on the validity of those proven to be correct by history and archeology. Even though many would agree with the validity of the accounts in books of the Bible like Amos, the first prophetic book of the Bible, the unbelieving can be assured that "truthfulness" in these reports are a high priority.

In the Old Testament, the book of Ezekiel in chapter 7, resonates with the theme: "The End Has Come". Does that mean an apocalypse hit Israel like the apocalypse of the flood in Noah's time? Not exactly, but Jeremiah (the prophet in the book of Jeremiah) started prophesying roughly 25 years before Ezekiel that Israel and Judah would be taken in Babylonian exile for 70 years. His prophecy was accurately fulfilled. Ezekiel, as a young man, followed in Jeremiah's footsteps. Ezekiel was used by God to let Israel and Judah know that their way of life is over. The average Israelite didn't want hard times, but it was upon them.

Only a fool would want a bad economy or civil unrest or a major catastrophe. If a person is looking for the coming of the Messiah, then many people wouldn't call them crazy. Based on prophecy, it's very likely that famine, wars and natural disasters will accompany that time period, but the person looking for the Messiah does not desire hard times.

Ezekiel and the citizens of Israel didn't want their way of life to be over, but they had entered a time of continued rebellion toward their traditions and "higher calling" in their society and personal lives. Israel continued to rebel and go their own way, regardless of God's blessings through many generations (including the many accounts found in the book of Judges). Israel reached a point where God didn't give them an alternative. Not to be trite, but there is coming a day when there will be no choice for "an alternative life style" in America. Ezekiel 7:1-3 (NIV) says, "The word of the Lord came to me, this is what the Sovereign Lord says to the land of Israel: The end! The end has come upon the four corners of the land. The end is now upon you and I will unleash my anger upon you". Read the rest of Ezekiel 7. You will be amazed how this chapter parallels Revelation 20:13 and Romans 2:6.

Israel had a lot of sins, but one of the main ones was idolatry. One of the main tenets of the Jewish and Christian faith is found in the first commandment of the Ten Commandments, "You shall have no other gods before me". The second commandment says, "You shall not make for yourself an idol in the form of anything ".... (Exodus 20:3,4). The people of Israel trampled the Ten Commandments and other commandments of God, like they trampled their grapes in preparation for making wine.

God warned them for many generations about their rebellion and pagan practices. Finally, through Ezekiel, God gave them their final warning, and told Israel that His Glory was going to depart from the Temple. Chapter 10 of Ezekiel is the dramatic account of God's glory departing from the temple in Jerusalem. Ezekiel 10 is even more impressive than the most eloquent scene written in "Paradise Lost" by John Milton. The following is part of the passage from Ezekiel 10:15-19: "When the cherubim moved, the wheels beside them moved; and when the cherubim spread their wing to rise from the ground, the wheels did not leave their side...Then the glory of the Lord departed from over the threshold of the temple and stopped above the cherubim".

When God's glory left the Temple in Jerusalem, it symbolized that God's glory and protection had left all of Israel and Judah (Israel split into Israel and Judah after the reign of King Solomon). No history even comes close to the longevity and thoroughness of the recorded history of Israel and its people. Even though the Bible records history many generations before Noah and the flood, the beginning of

Israel's history goes back to Abraham; about 4,000 years ago. (Genesis 12) Jeremiah and Ezekiel prophesied that Babylon would conquer and take the Israelites. Babylon (the leading power of its day) placed the Israelites into captivity between 600 B.C. and 580 B.C.

Can the United States learn a valuable lesson from Jewish history? America could learn from the mistakes of the Israelites, but it's doubtful that America will. It's true that many citizens of the United States believe in the historical record of the Bible and God, who the Jewish people called "I AM". In Hebrew God is spelled, "YHWH" and pronounced "Yahweh". Christians refer to the God of creation and the God of the Old Testament and New Testament, most commonly as God, Lord or Father. Christians refer to Christ, most commonly as Jesus, Jesus Christ or the Son of God, and as Messiah.

Individual Americans have learned not only lessons from the Israelites but from the Bible as a whole. Churches and Synagogues appreciate the meaning and lessons of the Bible. The United States Constitution guarantees us freedom of religion and speech, and our founding fathers had the greatest intentions of giving us the liberty of freedom of religion and speech. The problem in America is not that we have freedom for different religions, but that the Supreme Court has misinterpreted the intent our founding fathers had for separation of church and state. Our founding fathers for the most part were Christians. Benjamin Franklin was a deist, but he still revered God and valued God's direction. The vast majority of our founding fathers were Christian, including the father of our country, George Washington.

Our country was founded on Christian principles. John Adams, the second president of the United States and signer of the Declaration of Independence said, "The general principles on which the Fathers achieved independence were the general principles of Christianity... I have examined all religions and the result is that the Bible is the best book in the world". The death of John Adams and Thomas Jefferson, the author of the Declaration of Independence and third President of the United States, is more than a coincidence. They both died on July 4, 1826, exactly 50 years after they both signed The Declaration of Independence. Today's world has secular countries, Muslim countries, Hindu countries, Buddhist countries and communist countries.

The United States was a Christian country, but many Christians feel that "the glory of God has departed". Separation of Church and State was not created to segregate religion from schools and government practices, but it was created by our founding fathers to avoid a Theocracy that was common in Europe. Theocracies allowed religious practices to rule the government. The countries had a king, but the religion of the countries helped rule the government. In America it's ridiculous to think that the United Methodist Church or the Southern Baptists or the Catholics would help rule America.

Our founding fathers wanted to make sure that didn't happen here, but the humanists and the left wing radicals have influenced Congress and the Supreme Court to keep prayer, the Ten Commandments and readings from the scriptures out of schools and government. Our founding fathers never intended for prayer and scripture to be kept out of schools and the government. If they had known how secular or humanistic the American government would have become, they would have probably invoked laws stating that prayer and scripture cannot be removed from schools and government. In early America the McGuffey Reader was the country's main reading primer, and there was a quotation from the Bible on most every page.

America was not founded by communists, Buddhists, Hindus, or Muslims. America was founded as a Christian country, where Christian and Jewish beliefs were respected, protected and practiced. America is a country of freedom. Freedom of speech and religion are valued highly. Other religions have freedom of religion in America. America did not invite other religions or humanistic beliefs to change our country. Humanists and the radical left changed the United States into a socialist and secular country. If our founding fathers would have known about organizations like the ACLU, they would have outlawed them.

Our founding fathers would understand and many traditional Americans today understand why "the glory has departed". There is a large segment of America's population today that says "we are going to take back our country". They are saying that they have had enough of the philosophies and practices of humanism and socialism from the radical left. They are praying that God will change the direction of the United States, and they are proclaiming "In God We Trust".

The author is writing these words just a few days before Christmas of 2015. In Church this morning, we sang "Joy to the World". The music was written by Handel who wrote "The Hallelujah Chorus". The beginning of the last verse struck a familiar chord, "He rules the world with truth and grace, and makes the nations prove The glories of His righteousness, and wonders of His love".

There is a black mark on America today. Slavery was a grave aberration for America, and Native Americans are still suffering from how they've been treated for over 150 years. Today America is making the greatest mistake that they've made in the last 47 years: legalized abortion. Since the Supreme Court of the United States made abortion legal through their decision of Roe vs. Wade, America has gone downhill. Has the glory departed?

Hitler was responsible for 17 million deaths; Stalin for 23 million deaths; Mao Tse-Tung for at least 50 million deaths and American endorsers of legalized abortion for over 60 million deaths. When American Human Rights advocates slap the hands of China, North Korea, Iran and other countries for their absence of human rights, it is like the pot calling the kettle black.

Most abortions are practiced for convenience. The most common argument for legalized abortion is for the safety of the mother, incest and rape. Abortion does not have to be legal for medical professionals to get permission to save a mother's life. Well over 95% of the abortions are unnecessary. In the last 47 years, over 57 million lives could have been saved if the United States had not allowed legal abortion. How can a so-called "educated" country allow this insane genocide? The generation of the Great Depression called them "educated fools". For decades I've referred to them as pseudo-intellectuals, but the generation of the Great Depression is more accurate with their description of "educated fools".

There are probably several reasons why the glory has departed from America, but if legal abortion is revoked, will the glory return to America? Only God knows. With faith in God and following the ways of God, there is always hope.

Chapter Six

UFOs and Lost Files

One could say that UFOs have more to do with science fiction than with science! The author doesn't disagree, but it's far less interesting to write about the apocalypse without mentioning good science fiction like "War of the Worlds", "The Day the Earth Stood Still" and "2001, A Space Odyssey" (which I saw the premier in Hollywood, California in June of 1968; the only time I've been in Hollywood). While I'm venting good science fiction, humor me while I vent the magical sounds I heard when I was a young kid: Buddy Holly, Elvis, Ritchie Valens, The Platters, The Everly Brothers, Chuck Berry and Jerry Lee Lewis!

I've met people who make comments like, "what is the meaning of all of this talk about UFOs!" Seriously, it does deserve some attention. As an older kid in the 1960s, I use to tease my dad about his belief in UFOs (at some point all kids think they're smarter than their parents). My dad read books by a local UFO author (Frank Edwards), who was also an anchor on one of the Indianapolis TV channels. My dad would go out at times on a clear evening and look for UFOs. You might guess it; he never saw one. I didn't believe in them, but I saw one on October 23, 1973. People might wonder how I kept my sanity all of these years; I didn't make it public! I have shared it with a lot of family and friends through the years. I think and hope that most people believe me.

Some people who have listened to my experience, want to know what I think about all of the UFO sightings. Like most people, I have my own theory. Having the experience of seeing one didn't keep me awake at nights, but I was shook up the first couple hours after I saw one. In later 1973, I was working with two other ministers, Dale Workman from Indiana and Larry Williams from Oklahoma. We went to a revival meeting one evening during the week in Dayton, Ohio. After the meeting, we were traveling the interstate out of Dayton to go back to Indiana, on a clear, cool October evening between 10:30 and 11 pm. The traffic was very light and the night sky so clear, we could see a lot of stars even while we traveled in Larry's little Toyota Corolla (remember those!) Being the youngest and skinniest of the three (at that time), I was riding in the back seat while Larry and Dale rode in the front seats.

At the same time, we looked out of the front windshield, and all three of us in unison said, "look there!" In front us, we saw a phenomenal sight that appeared to be outside of our atmosphere. It looked like a huge, orange star, that seemed to be larger than what one would envision the Bethlehem star to be. Within a minute it seemed to come in from outside the atmosphere to along the highway, where we were traveling. Larry pulled off at the next exit, and we came back to the Englewood exit and back on the interstate, where we saw the UFO getting close to us. We saw the UFO stop in midair, about 15 yards over a tree line, that ran parallel to the highway. The bright object pulled forward about 20 to 30 yards, then it stopped again in midair; we heard no sounds.

Larry pulled over on the shoulder, and he immediately jumped out to try to get closer to the UFO. Even though I was shaking like Don Knots, I jumped out and ran after Larry. I was right behind Larry when he climbed over a fence to get even closer. I started to climb over, when I said, "where is it, Larry?" He said, "I don't know; it just disappeared". It just vanished; no trace of sound or sight.

I had the three of us draw our own pictures and write our own report of what we saw. All of us saw how it came in; it's very brilliant dome and saucer shape. Larry or Dale thought they saw little windows in the dome. The light was so bright coming out of the dome that I just saw the brightness. Aliens are also colorful beings, because I saw a green light and a red light under the UFO! When we got back to Muncie, I called the local state trooper's office. It was around midnight, and the trooper on duty said that an agency in Arizona had taken over the UFO investigations from the Air Force. He gave me the Arizona address, and I mailed our report the next day. About two to three weeks later, I received a letter in the mail from the Arizona agency. They said that our sighting was an official UFO sighting, and they assured us that it was not any United States or Russian aircraft.

There have been more UFO sighting, since sightings in the fifties and sixties. I was curious about any sightings near the date of our sighting. Six days before our sighting, on October 17, 1973, the Duke Field radar unit with Eglin Air Force Base in Florida tracked UFOs, while 10 to 15 people saw four UFOs flying between Milton and Crestview, Florida, along I10. We also saw a UFO come alongside an interstate. On October 23, a Holiday Inn was being constructed at the Englewood Exit, on the outskirts of Dayton. Only the shell of the building was up; the roof had not yet been built. Near the Englewood Exit was Wright-Patterson Air Force Base!

Some UFO investigators say that it is common for UFOs to fly along energy sources, like airports, nuclear power plants and fault lines. I'm not convinced that the energy source report is the reason for UFO appearances. They also fly in many other areas. In the 1990s, when personal computers became very popular, authors and celebrities would have 20 to 30-minute question and answer sessions. A known author of UFOs, who was versed on UFOs as well as anyone in the nineties, had a 25-minute session one day on the internet. The participants could type up to 10 questions and send them to the author.

The session was almost over, when the author answered my first question. He believed that Satan (or the father of this world according to the Bible) was manifesting appearances of UFOs by opening up the fourth dimension. He felt that Satan knew we were getting closer to apocalyptic days, and he was trying everything possible to distract the minds of mankind from the things of God. Albert Einstein would have certainly agreed with the UFO author about the possibility of a fourth dimension.

Does the possible increase of activities of a real Satan and demons give additional signs to the proximity of the apocalypse – absolutely! C.S. Lewis made these comments about "spiritual wickedness in high places" (Ephesians 6:12), "There are two mistakes a Christian can make about demons. One is not to believe in them at all. The other mistake is to believe in them and have an unhealthy, that is to say, too much interest in them".

Is it more than coincidence that there has been more UFO activity, since the 1970s? In April of 1973 there was also a very clear UFO sighting along the New Madrid fault line. An officer from Piedmont, Missouri, saw the UFO. Also, two state troopers saw a UFO up close near the Pennsylvania state line along Route 224. They also saw the UFO suddenly take off. There have been over 300 sightings along the Rio Grande Rift, which is in Colorado, New Mexico and Mexico, by 2011. The reports of UFO sightings since the 1970s seem to be never ending.

Former President Jimmy Carter saw a UFO, and former President Bill Clinton has looked into UFO reports extensively. One of many reports of the frequency of UFO sightings since the 1970s comes from the western Piedmont of North Carolina. The following report was from The Augusta Chronicle, from May 18, 1997: "The western Piedmont has had a reputation for frequent UFO sightings since the early

1970s. On October 24, 1973, more than 50 people including Surry County Sheriff's deputies, reported strange lights from Shoals to Mount Airy". The frequency of the sightings has been so great since the seventies that UFO followers guess that only one out of ten UFO sightings are reported.

No doubt that between unreported sightings, the Air Force and Area 51, there are many lost files. The lost files give credence to the abundance of reported and unreported UFO sightings since the 1970s. Besides the increase of frequency of UFO sightings, are there any other parallels that connect UFO encounters with the proximity of apocalyptic events? C.S. Lewis was not only a great Christian author, but he was also a gifted philosopher. Think again about his quote concerning spiritual wickedness in high places. The first part of his statement says, "There are two mistakes that Christians can make about demons. One is not to believe in them at all". Even though most scientists dismiss reports of UFO sightings, and don't have an interest in investigating them, the mistake is not to believe in them at all. Since there is a great abundance of sightings, it is a mistake not to believe in them. Secondly, the second part of the C.S. Lewis quote is, "The other mistake is to believe in them and have an unhealthy, that is to say, too much interest in them".

It's not necessary for science to have a great interest in investigating UFOs, but believing that they exist is wise. Patrick J. Kiger with the "National Geographic Channel" reported "Five Good Reasons to Believe in UFOs": "1. The long, documented history of sightings. 2. Numerous modern sightings by credible, well-trained professional observers. 3. Consistencies in the description of purported alien ships. 4. Possible, physical evidence of encounters with alien spacecraft. 5. Physiological effects on UFO witnesses".

C.S. Lewis is right. It's a mistake to not believe in them at all. Demons are real and UFOs are real, but too much interest in them is unhealthy. His reasoning is correct. Through the last 43 years, I have kept my sanity about UFOs based on that type of rationale: I believe in them, but I don't think much about them! The Christian author of UFOs is also correct. There are a lot of things that distract people from the things of God. To name a few along with UFOs are: greed, materialism, pornography, unnatural affection, lust, deceit, man-made religions, delusions of grandeur, false witness, crime, fabrication, violence, prejudice, false judgments, vanity, selfishness, anger, pride and rebellion; to name a few.

There is possibly a logical reason for the existence of UFOs. Obviously, people are attracted to the aircraft; the way it looks and the way it operates. The fascination was portrayed well in "Close Encounters of the Third Kind", especially when the UFO landed on Devil's Tower. I've always been thankful for God's creation that we know about, and I've wondered about God's creation, that we don't know about.

Why hasn't man been able to enter the fourth dimension or travel at the speed of light? We've learned from Einstein that these feats are possible, yet man hasn't accomplished them. Why hasn't man been able to develop aircraft like the UFOs that have been so frequently witnessed to? We don't find indications of crafts like bicycles, motorcycles, cars, trucks, trains and airplanes in the Bible. Yet, we do find more than one very likely accounts of UFOs in the Bible.

Years ago I listened to several church leaders read the account of Elijah being taken to heaven. Elisha, who took Elijah's place as Israel's prophet, was walking along with Elijah, who had performed many miracles during his tenure as Israel's prophet. 2 Kings 2:11 (NIV) records, "As they were walking along and talking together, suddenly a chariot of fire and horses of fire appeared and separated the two of them, and Elijah went up to heaven in a whirlwind". This is a recorded event from roughly 3,000 years ago. At that time, without MP3s, tape recorders or cameras, it is probably the most accurate account that could be given that time of a UFO.

Elijah was Israel's main prophet in the 9th century B.C. He is one of mankind's main spiritual leaders. Enoch was the only other person to be taken directly to heaven without experiencing death. Elijah ministered to Israel between the reign of Solomon and the Babylonian captivity. Ezekiel was Israel's main prophet immediately before the Babylonian exile and during the captivity. Elijah was not the only Israelite to experience a close encounter of the third kind (Elisha also witnessed the phenomena). Ezekiel witnessed a similar phenomenon over 200 years after Elijah was taken to heaven.

Ezekiel 1 gives another witness of a close encounter: "Fire moved back and forth among the creatures; it was bright, and lightning flashed out of it. The creature sped back and forth like flashes of lightning. As I looked at the living creatures, I saw a wheel on the ground beside each creature with its four faces... Each appeared to be made like a wheel intersecting a wheel. As they moved they would go in any one of the four directions the creatures face; the wheels did not turn about as the creatures went". (Ezekiel 1:12-18 NIV)

Ezekiel 10:6-19 gives another account of a close encounter that Ezekiel had when the glory of God departed from the Temple at Jerusalem: "When the Lord commanded the man in linen, take fire from among the wheels, from among the cherubim, the man went in and stood beside a wheel... I looked, and I saw beside the cherubim; the wheels, one beside each of the cherubim; the wheels sparkled like chrysolite.... each was like a wheel intersecting a wheel. As they moved, they would go in any one of the four directions the cherubim face; the wheels did not turn about as the cherubim went... I heard the wheels being called "the whirlwind wheels". A skeptic might say that the accounts don't prove they were

UFOs. What were they then – a car, train or airplane? They sound like a UFO; not a car, train or plane.

The reported UFO accounts in 1Kings and Ezekiel may very well be a creation of God that we know very little about. It's strange that man hasn't invented this type of craft, if it were meant to be. It may not be a scientific hypothesis, but I have my own theological hypothesis: if the end as we know it is upon us, then we're running out of time to invent a UFO type craft. If the author were a betting person, would he bet on the invention of the UFO craft first or the events of the apocalypse first? No doubt, he would bet on the latter.

Chapter Seven

The Six Millenniums

A large portion of the people that have lived since the dawn of mankind are alive today. At the birth of Christ, about 200 to 300 million people lived on the earth. In 1650 about 500 million people were living on earth, and in 1800 the earth's population was just over 1 billion. At the end of 2015, almost 7.4 billion people were living in the world! In 2,000 BC the world population was an estimated 25 million! Today the earth supports about 300 times the number of people than in 2,000 BC!

Once again consumption is a big issue approaching the apocalypse. Depletion of natural resources, land, clean air, trees, plants, animals and water, is one of the world's biggest problems; much more than climate change! Jesus Christ addressed the issue of famine in the last days. Did Jesus point us toward a future time when the world as we know it would end?

2,000 years ago (2 millenniums), Jesus told his disciples, "But about that day and hour no one knows, not even the angels in heaven, nor the Son, but only the Father". (Matthew 24:36 NIV) Notice that Jesus didn't say the year! Many people have tried to predict the year, but so far all have failed. Obviously, any future prediction is a possibility, but it's open to failure too. It's important to remember that a day is like a thousand years to God, and that a thousand years are like a day.

No one can argue that the year 1999 has passed, but has the significance of 1999 passed? There was a prediction as well as a possible spiritual connection that will blow your mind. First of all, let's look at three heavy weights in the field of predictions. First of all, Jesus Christ is the all-time champion prophet, because He is the Son of God! Secondly, even though Nostradamus and Edgar Cayce were occasionally wrong, they have been right so many times about significant events that it is uncanny.

Edgar Cayce has been correct about major events like World War II and the Great Depression. He also accurately predicted the deaths of Franklin D. Roosevelt and John F. Kennedy. In 1932 Cayce predicted the reoccurrence of Israel as a nation, which happened after World War II in 1948. Cayce's clients included Thomas Edison, Woodrow Wilson, George Gershwin and Irving Berlin. Cayce also helped many people with health problems. He had no formal medical training, but while he was in a mental trance he could describe medically the most complicated surgeries and medical diagnoses that only skilled surgeons and professionals are familiar with.

Even though Cayce didn't profit from the advice he gave, many investors became wealthy during 20 years of a Bull Market before the Great Depression from Cayce's counsel. It is almost unbelievable that Cayce, who lived from 1877 to 1945, and Nostradamus, who lived from 1503 to 1566, predicted the same year for the return of Christ! Nostradamus was also correct about many significant events. He predicted feats that came true about Napoleon, the World Wars, the burning of the twin towers and many other significant events. In his era, no one came close to predicting the future as accurately as Nostradamus.

While Nostradamus opened the future for people during and after his time, Martin Luther, during the same time period, was opening up the Bible, God's will and the spiritual future for people during and after his time. It's amazing that during the time of the great Nostradamus (in France), that in his neighboring country of Germany, Martin Luther, the father of The Reformation, was at work liberating people spiritually.

Martin Luther and Nostradamus both lived to be 62 1/2 years. Luther lived from 1483 to 1546 and Nostradamus from 1503 to 1566. They were both working prolifically in the 1520s and the 1530s. Nostradamus may not have known that he was virtually rubbing shoulders with the founder of The Reformation, and Nostradamus did probably not know that 350 years after his lifetime, Edgar Cayce would be following in his footsteps.

Both Cayce and Nostradamus predicted that Christ would return in the year 1999! Most people would react by saying that they were both emphatically wrong about the time of Christ's return, but is there a spiritual connection? What about Christ's prophecy that he would return before the generation passed away, when the branch of the fig tree was young and tender? Almost all reputable Biblical scholars agree that the passages about the fig tree in the Bible, represent Israel.

Israel had not been a nation since 70 AD, and the world was amazed that almost 1400 years later, Israel became a nation again in 1948! My brother was born in 1944 and 71 years later, he is still working. In 1999, he was a young 55-year-old. Since the predictions of Cayce and Nostradamus carry a lot of weight, what if the world just doesn't know about the spiritual side of the return of Christ. In 1975, I remember a number of reports about many people witnessing heavenly hosts hovering over Jerusalem.

In 1932, Cayce predicted that Israel would be a nation again. How many other people in 1932 would have believed that Israel would be a nation just three years after World War II ended? Cayce predicted the event even six years before Hitler and the Nazis started invading other countries. Skeptics might not believe Cayce and Nostradamus about the return of Christ, but it could happen any day.

Jesus said that He would return as a thief in the night, when people are not expecting him. He said to be prepared (also a good message for the preppers and non-preppers). There are many studies by so-called modern day prophets about the return of Christ. There are some logical reasons based on scriptures that the year could be 2030 or another year (according to some), but the bottom line is that is he coming as a "thief in the night"! People are still predicting all kinds of time periods for Christ's return, but He told us to be prepared. He could return any day; at any moment.

Concerning the last days and the return of Christ, it's wise to look at the six millenniums before the year 2,000 AD. The first millennium we're looking at is from Adam to Noah. The second millennium is from Noah to Abraham, and the third is from Abraham to David. The fourth millennium is from David to Christ. The fifth millennium is from the time of Christ to the early dark ages in 1,000 AD, and the sixth millennium is from 1,000 AD to 2,000 AD. We are now in the seventh millennium!

The gospel of Luke, a talented physician, researcher and author, recorded man's ancestry from the beginning! The oral and written tradition of the pre-Israelites; the Israelites and later the Jewish people, Is of great importance to them like their religion. In Luke 3:23-38, we find the complete ancestry from Adam to Jesus. From Adam to Noah, Luke records ten generations. From Shem, Noah's son, to Abraham, Luke records eleven generations. From Isaac, Abraham's son, to David, Luke records thirteen generations. From Nathan, David's son, to Jesus, Luke records 42 generations. Let's run the math.

There are about 1,000 years and ten generations from Adam to Noah, tradition says that Methuselah, Noah's grandfather knew Adam! Of course, Methuselah also knew Noah! Tradition also says that Noah's son, Shem, also knew

Abraham! But there were also about 1,000 years and 42 generations between David and Jesus. Why are there so many more generations between David and Jesus; most people in Jesus' day lived to about 40 and Adam lived to be 930 and Noah to 950 years. The oldest person ever was Noah's grandfather, Methuselah, who lived to be 969 years old! After the flood, God told Noah that man's day would be up to 120 years.

Abraham and his wife Sara were two of the last people to live well over the age of 120. Sara lived to be 127 and Abraham lived to be 175. In Christ's day it was common for people to die between the ages of 35 and 40. In the 1800s, a lot of people survived to age 58. The average life expectancy in the United States today is almost 79.

Several years ago, a research team stated that the baby boomers would be the last generation to live the longest (in this millennium and in comparison, to the last millennium). Their main reasoning was the great increase of the toxins in the air, water and ground. (Of course, an impending apocalypse could also confirm that theory.) Since World War II, the toxins keep accumulating. It is true that man has always polluted the environment from fires to forging to manufacturing lead and other metals, but the nature of the pollutants today is far more dangerous.

Newer toxins today are not only polluting the environment, but they are accumulating in the environment, because they are not biodegradable. Included in these very toxic chemicals are: plastics, PCBs and inorganic pesticides. Toxins cause an increased rate in cancer, birth defects, autism, mental and physical disabilities and other health problems. The author knows of a documented case where two young brothers developed autism, because there was wood treated with arsenic that had been buried around their family's organic garden.

Toxins are not only adversely affecting humans, but plants and animals as well. Of Course, hazardous waste and industrial spills add to the mounting problem. Dirty air, water and land escalate the shortages of healthy food and water, and they escalate the hazards of pandemics. Some medical professionals think the discovery of new drugs, including new antibiotics, will help the younger generations live longer. Unfortunately, countries and their engineers and manpower cannot keep up with all of the pollution problems in the air, water and ground. Many American cities have not been able to keep up with addressing widespread sewage problems. In the middle of China's industrial revolution, the Chinese and the world are experiencing some of the greatest pollution problems in history.

There are thousands more of different chemicals in the world today than during World War II. In most men's and women's bathroom products, there are hazardous materials. In most food, there are additives, preservatives and other unhealthy products. Toxins accumulate in the body and eventually in the brain. They can cause tumors, cancer, Alzheimer's, multiple sclerosis, many other diseases and death. Supervised Chelation therapy or obtaining over the counter or mail order natural chelators can remove a lot of the heavy metal and toxic build-up in the human body.

Just from the facts of "the toxic world", it sounds like mankind is doomed, without mentioning all the other potential disasters! Now and then, the History Channel runs a program called the "Prophets of Doom". They are six conscientious and intelligent men who each have their own take on what will happen to the world. Of course, they don't want an apocalypse, but they point out what the world is coming to (from six different points of view). One of the men on the panel says that his concern is real "when we've seen so many apocalyptic problems on the horizon".

How much does the sixth (and last full millennium as we know it) as well as the current (seventh millennium) tell us about what we're facing in the very near future? It's worth the endeavor to also take a brief look at the first five millenniums as well. Some educator's complicate fields of history, theology, archeology and sociology with skepticism and cynicism. A number of subjects are not nearly so complicated as some so-called educators make them.

There is a lot of speculation on the part of historians, geologists and archeologists about the age of man. Scholars do agree that the cradle of civilization is known as the Sumerian civilization. Historians and archeologists believe that the Sumerians emerged about 6,000 years ago with the first written language. The ancient Sumerians were located in southern Iraq. Is it coincidence that the Garden of Eden was also located in the same general area?

In Genesis 2:10-14, the scripture records the location of the Garden of Eden. The passage says that a river flowed out of Eden to water the garden and from there it divided into four rivers: The Pishon River; the Gihon River, the Tigris River and the Euphrates River. Today the Tigris and Euphrates sources flow out of the Taurus mountains of eastern Turkey. The Euphrates River flows through part of Turkey and Syria and joins the Tigris River in southern Iraq then flows into the Persian Gulf.

Since the scientists of archeology know that the Sumerians were a civilization 6,000 years ago, that would have given the lineage from Adam and Eve time to expand and become a civilization in the same general land area of Sumer in 1,000 years or less! The other most common references to ancient civilizations are the peoples of Mesopotamia. Mesopotamia included most of modern day Iraq and parts of Syria, Turkey and Iran.

It is also more than coincidental that Abram (who became Abraham and the beginning of Israel) was also from the same geographic area. Abraham was from the City of Ur, which was part of Chaldea. Chaldea was the southern region of Sumer, and later Chaldea was absorbed into the country of Babylonia (now southern Iraq).

It is no wonder that the first known, written words came from the cradle of civilization, the Sumerians. Southern Sumer, Chaldea, was inhabited by a Semitic tribe. Even though some scholars think that the beginning of the Bible in written word was around 1300 BC, it is likely that the ancestors of Abraham started recording the events in Genesis long before 1300 BC. There may have been some written work in Sumer as far back as 3000 BC or before.

Jews are emphatic (and probably right) about the accuracy of their oral tradition, since the time of Adam, Noah and Abraham. There also could have been cuneiform records long before the time that most Jews and other religious people realize. Most Christians are definitely emphatic about the accuracy of the Old and New Testaments. Muslims, Mormons and Jehovah's Witnesses also base some of their religions on parts of the Bible.

The first millennium, from Adam to Noah, would be exhilarating to experience. The only survivors to experience the Garden of Eden were Adam and Eve; what a story that would be! Even though the Bible more than any other source, gives the best thorough account of mankind before 2,000 BC, there is not a lot of information about man between the early years of Adam and the early years of Noah. We know that after Cain killed Abel, Adam and Eve had a son named Seth. Cain also had a son named Enoch. We also know that Cain had descendants that made tools out of bronze and iron, and we know Cain built a city. From the Biblical record, we know there were a little more than a 1,000 years between the time of Adam and Noah.

The second millennium, like the first millennium, tells us about faith or man's religion much more than about science. Man continued to advance in knowledge and weapons of war, but his scientific knowledge did not develop much until the fifth and sixth millenniums. One of the most significant scriptures from the second millennium for mankind today is from Genesis 6:13 (NIV)," So God said to Noah, "I am going to put an end to all people, for the earth is filled with violence because of them. I am surely going to destroy both them and the earth".

There is also a significant scripture from the fifth millennium that connects the second millennium to current time! Luke 17:26 and Matthew 24:37-39 refer to how the last days will be similar to the time of Noah in the second millennium: "As it was in the days of Noah, so it will be at the coming of the Son of Man. For in the days before the flood, people were eating and drinking, marrying and giving in marriage, up to the day Noah entered the ark; and they knew nothing about what would happen until the flood came and took them all away".... The days of Noah in the second millennium; the days of Christ in the fifth millennium and our current days at the beginning of the seventh millennium have a common denominator: God, the deliverer! Also, God was the deliverer in the third millennium during the time of Joseph and Moses.

During the early days of the Israelites, before they were a nation, God delivered them from famine through Joseph, who was in Egypt at that time. (Genesis 47 and 48) God also delivered people who followed him during the time of Moses in the third millennium. (Exodus 7-13) After the generation of Joseph died, the new king of Egypt did not know about Joseph and how he came to power. Exodus 1 says that the Israelites continued to multiply and came to have a large population. Because the new king feared their great number and what they could potentially do, he oppressed them and put them into forced labor.

    Hollywood and other producers have probably made as many movies about Noah and about Moses as they have about Christ. The movie media portrays the significance of God's delivering power in the time of Noah, Moses and Christ. Noah and his family were delivered by God from the flood in the second millennium; the Israelites in Egypt were delivered from oppression by God through Moses in the third millennium; Christ delivered the world from evil for the people who followed Him in the fifth millennium and those millenniums to follow. The author is not predicting the hour, day or even the year of Christ's return, but he is predicting that it will be in the seventh millennium during the current generation.

    It's important to reflect that God is the creator: of the earth, the sky, the land, the sea, plants and animals. He is also the creator of love, good will, peace, intelligence, talents, art, music, creativeness and many other things. ("He" is gender neutral: scriptures say that there is no male nor female in heaven.) We are created in His image. He has given us the ability to think and to create. He has given us the ability to have language, a number system and advances in education.

    Think about his perfect number (as proven in the Bible), the number seven. We are in the seventh millennium. God delivered Noah and his family in the second millennium. God delivered Joseph, Moses and their people in the third millennium. Christ first delivered people of the fifth millennium, and we are now in the seventh millennium. Look at the millennial numbers:2-3-5-7. You don't have to be a follower of astrology to be a numbers person. Mathematicians and statisticians are numbers people. Think of yourself as an amateur mathematician. 2-3-5-7 ends with the perfect number "7". Add the four numbers:2+3+5+7="17". Look at the sequence: "1" is skipped; then "4" is skipped; then "6" is skipped. The first millennium was God's beginning for man. The fourth and fifth millenniums were for growth and the seventh millennium is the conclusion. In any speech, letter or book, there is an opening, a body of content and a conclusion. We are living in the conclusion.

The third millennium begins with the life of Abraham. Two people that should be studied in all history books today are Jesus and Abraham. We already know why Jesus is the most important person in history: He changed the world! It's unfortunate that many modern day historians seem oblivious to the most important relationships of people with the world. Abraham is also in the very top of the list of the most important people in history. He is revered by Jews, Christians and Muslims. To the Jews, Abraham is the father of Israel (the person as well as the nation of Israel). God changed the name of Isaac (Abraham's son) to Israel.

To the Muslims, Abraham, is their early ancestor as well. Abraham's first son, Ishmael, was birthed by Hagar, Abraham's handmaiden (by consent of his wife, so Abraham would have a child). Muslim's ancestry is from Ishmael. Unfortunately, Hagar and Ishmael were told to leave Abraham's camp, because there was conflict that stemmed from Ishmael and Isaac (Abraham's second son, who Sarah bore). Spiritually, one can try to understand why there has been a conflict from these two ancestral lines since the third millennium.

One reason Muslim based nations are not allied as close to Israel as Christian based nations is the Bible. Jewish beliefs are mainly based on the Torah (the Pentateuch, the first five books of the Bible: Genesis through Deuteronomy). Jews do revere other books in the Old Testament like the Torah.

Muslims do not revere most of the Bible, whereas Christians revere the Old and the New Testaments of the Bible. One could say that Christians also consider Abraham an ancestor as well, but more of a spiritual ancestor. The line of Christ does extend from Adam to Noah to Abraham to David and to Christ. (Luke 3:23-38) Christ did not have children, including Knights Templar descendants, and he wasn't married to Mary Magdalene, and He didn't have a sexual relationship with any woman (read Matthew, Mark, Luke and John of the New Testament). For those who know what I'm speaking of: it's amazing that lies/myths can sell 40 million books!

The beginnings of the nation of Israel grew through the third millennium. Isaac had twins, Esau and Jacob. These two brothers had an even greater conflict! No doubt that their ancestors are in conflict with each other today. Jacob had twelve sons, who became the twelve tribes of Israel. Joseph was the most famous. He was sold into slavery by his brothers, but he became a great power in Egypt and a deliverer of his family. The line of Christ though continued through Judah rather than Joseph (which is interesting, because Joseph was a type of Christ by the life he lived). The Israelites grew so numerous in Egypt that Moses led them on their exodus. The Ten Commandments were given to the Israelites and later to the Gentiles through Moses during the exodus.

Joshua took Moses place, and entered Canaan Land, and conquered many of the Canaanite cities and tribes. The twelve tribes were given their allotments of land, and were governed by judges after a rough beginning. Approaching the fourth millennium, the Israelites wanted a king, and God had Saul anointed as King of Israel. At that time the coastal Canaanites, the Philistines, were Israel's main enemy (but not their only enemy). David ushered in the fourth millennium and replaced Saul as King of Israel. David fought a lot of battles and had much to overcome, but by the end of David's reign, Israel was a strong nation.

David's son, Solomon, replaced David as King of Israel. God blessed Solomon with the gift of wisdom, and under Solomon's reign, Israel became a prominent nation and highly respected. Israel's earthly glory as a nation was during the reign of Solomon during the dawn of the fourth millennium.

After Solomon's reign, it was mostly downhill for Israel as a nation. Solomon's two sons, Rehoboam and Jeroboam, ended up ruling a divided nation: Jeroboam over Israel (the ten northern tribes and Rehoboam over Judah). Much of Israel's history was lackluster after the reign of Solomon. Israel and Judah lost territory to their enemies, and about 450 years later, the Babylonians destroyed much of their cities and carried them into captivity in Babylon (back to the cradle of civilization, the general area where Abraham came from, the ancient city of Ur of Chaldea, in southern Sumer).

The Israelites didn't fare well during the remainder of the fourth millennium. They must have felt like they experienced two types of apocalypse. The first, in the fourth millennium, when they were relocated to Babylonia, where they lost their Hebrew language and much of their culture (but due to Jewish leaders like Ezekiel and Daniel, the Israelites preserved their religion, and were eventually restored to their homeland). Through the centuries, Israel was diminished to Palestine. About four centuries after they returned to their homeland, they were occupied by Rome.

Some historians say that Alexander the Great of Greece was the greatest, individual conqueror in history. He did conquer more land than any one person during his short life time. Rome was not a major power during his time. The major powers like Assyria and India were in the East. If Alexander the Great had started out conquering nearby Rome, undoubtedly, it would have significantly changed Roman history. In less than 100 years after Alexander's death, Rome conquered Greece.

The second type of apocalypse for Israel (now Palestine) came during the dawn of the fifth millennium, when Roman armies led by the Emperor's brother, General Titus (who later became Emperor) besieged Jerusalem. The beginnings of the siege were in 66 AD. Rome destroyed Jerusalem and the Second Temple in 70 AD, about thirty-seven years after Christ prophesied the destruction of Jerusalem. The Jews were devastated from the destruction of Jerusalem and the Second Temple (which was built after their return from Babylon). A million people were killed during the siege. The famous Jewish historian, Josephus, was wounded during the siege. Josephus was working for Rome as an historian and ambassador to Jerusalem at that time.

No doubt that the destruction of Jerusalem and the Temple was an early Holocaust for the Jews. It's phenomenal that Nostradamus predicted the demon by name of the World War II Holocaust, Hitler, about 1,400 years after the destruction of Jerusalem, and about 400 years before World War II. Only God could accomplish fulfilling a prophecy by Christ, almost 2,000 years after Jesus prophesied that Israel would be restored as a nation. If secular historians had their facts straight, the restoration of Israel would be one of the great wonders of all time! The world will soon go through a world-wide holocaust, but the author will soon share the good news for the faithful.

The birth of Christ marks the beginning of the fifth millennium. Time flies; we're almost through the last two, full millenniums and then it will be time for the return of Christ! A thousand years is as a day! The birth of Jesus is known as "The Greatest Story Ever Told". It's the greatest event of and for mankind. Being a history buff, it's sad that many modern day (humanist) historians, just don't get it.

As the greatest history book in the world, the Holy Bible, says, "He is called Emmanuel", because He is God with us. The beginning of the fifth millennium is the beginning of the end, with the birth and life of Jesus Christ. Jesus even said during His ministry that the end is near. His life is the new beginning for mankind. For the Jew, He is the Messiah that was promised by the old prophets. For the gentile (everyone else), he is the great hope and deliverer of mankind.

Even though much of the fifth millennium is called the "Dark Ages", it was the beginning and early growth of the church. The church spread throughout the known world for 300 years after the ministry of Christ, then King Constantine of the Eastern Roman Empire made Christianity a state religion. The Roman Catholic Church was formed 300 years after the church grew. The Roman Catholic Church had some great Christians through the centuries, like St. Augustine and St. Thomas Aquinas, but there was also a lot of corruption with leadership; their politics and executions for centuries.

Church history became fragmented through the Dark Ages. Both the Greek Orthodox Church and the Eastern Orthodox Church trace their roots to the apostolic age. The Christians and Messianic Jews in Ethiopia also trace their roots to the apostolic age. The Roman Catholic Church traces their roots back to the Apostle Peter. Yet, the Apostle Peter died between 67 AD and 68 AD, and the Roman Catholic Church was eventually established by 337 AD. Christians were given liberty in 313 AD by King Constantine when there was no catholic church, and the Roman Catholic Church was gradually established during the next twenty-five years.

The Protestant Reformation brought enlightenment to the church through Christian leaders like William Tyndale and Martin Luther. Leaders like Tyndale and Luther brought the

Bible, God's Word, to the people for the first time: An English Bible for the English, a German Bible for the Germans, etc. The common person learned from the Bible that Christians are justified by grace, and they are to practice love and forgiveness. The corrupt leaders in the Roman Catholic Church persecuted, jailed and executed many thousands of people. They excommunicated Martin Luther so they could execute him, but the German people protected Martin Luther.

Protestants are not without fault either. There have been many wonderful Christians in both the Protestant and Catholic churches. Jesus taught his people to forgive and not to judge. There were Jews who crucified Christ, but many Jews followed God's will and became followers of Christ. If they remained in the Jewish faith, it does not mean they didn't follow God's earlier commandments. Jesus taught, "He who is without sin, cast the first stone". Jesus, Reformation leaders, E. Stanley Jones, Martin Luther King, Billy Graham and many others have taught us to be peaceful and to forgive. Many Protestants and Catholics today are going throughout the world, sharing the good news of Christ and helping millions who are in need.

After Christ was crucified, risen and ascended to heaven and after the Roman Empire fell, the world was engulfed in the Dark Ages through most of the fifth millennium until mid-way into the sixth millennium. The 16th century brought not only the enlightenment of the Reformation to the world, but the 15th century ushered in the enlightenment of education to the world, especially the arts and sciences. We could take a whole book to discuss the advancements in science and industrialization, but we can sum it up it one word, spectacular! Thank God for the Reformation and the Renaissance! The Reformation and the Renaissance are evolved from a message of Christ: "Light shined into Darkness".

Before we conclude with the sixth millennium and open with the seventh, millennium, it's necessary to mention the apocalyptic type event of the sixth millennium. The bubonic plague was called "The Black Death". It killed about 25% of the world's population, and about half of Europe's population. Estimates vary widely from 100 to 200 million people killed. Most everyone has heard of the Black Death, but the Bubonic Plague was catastrophic on a scale to the flood during Noah's days.

It's true that the flood killed almost everyone, but the Black Death was just as horrific. Imagine two out of four people, who are near you, dying around the clock. It was also unimaginably troubling, because it didn't go away. It started in the early 14th century, and there were remnants of it into the 19th century. It kept reoccurring in England, Russia and other countries for several centuries. The bad news about the upcoming apocalypse is that there will be a world- wide pandemic, but the good news is that the total time of the great tribulation is seven years; not several centuries.

The sixth millennium was also plagued by wars (one of the prophecies of Christ in the end time, "wars and rumors of was"). There were too many to even try to mention all the major ones, but there were the wars of the Crusaders and the Muslims. There were the Napoleonic wars. There were the colonial wars like in India, Africa and America. There was the American Civil War that took more lives than all the other American wars put together, until the time of the Iraqi wars. Just imagine, we're near the end time and we're still fighting wars back in the cradle of civilization where the Sumerians and the Babylonians were from.

In America there were also the great wars of World War I and World War II, then America fought in South Korea. After South Korea, there was the terribly planned war in Viet Nam. Since Viet Nam, we've had two major wars in Iraq, and a long standing war in Afghanistan. As this is written (the first week of January, 2016), there is a major conflict between Saudi Arabia and Iran. At the same time, the stock market fell to its second lowest level since 2008. A prominent New York financial advisor and investor said that there would be a recession in the United States before the end of 2016.

The author's life, like other baby boomers, has taken him from the sixth millennium into the seventh millennium. Most baby boomers greatly preferred the culture of the fifties and sixties over a later, increasingly secular culture. Every generation has some differences as well. The baby boomers prefer Elvis, The Beatles and Chicago over Brittney Spears and Ice Cool Snoop LTL. Events of the young seventh millennium are already quite sobering.

The seventh millennium wasn't even two years old, when radical Islamic terrorists killed 3,000 Americans and destroyed the twin towers of the World Trade Center. Wars and terrorism have been two of the greatest problems in our new, seventh millennium.

"The Weather Channel" listed some of the worst natural disasters of the seventh millennium (since 2000 AD). In November, 2013, Typhoon Haiyan killed more than 10,000 people in the Philippines. A 9.0 Magnitude earthquake caused a tsunami off the coast of Japan on March 11, 2011. 19,000 people were killed, and there was a meltdown of three nuclear reactors.

After the 2010 earthquake in Haiti, my wife went with a medical team to aid in the Haitian relief efforts. A 7.0 earthquake heavily damaged Port-au-Prince, Haiti's capitol. About 200,000 people were killed in Haiti, and over 300,000 were injured. In 2008, a 7.9 earthquake killed 87,000 people in China. Cyclone Narglis in May of 2008, killed 138,000 people. In 2005, a 7.6 earthquake killed 80,000 people in Kashmir and Pakistan.

In 2004 a 9.1 earthquake and tsunami in Indonesia killed 230,000 people in twelve countries. In 2003 an earthquake in Iran killed 26,000 people.

Hurricane Katrina killed 1,000 people; one million people were displaced and New Orleans lost half of its population. Katrina caused $150 billion in damages.

It's depressing and almost impossible to list all of the disasters, including floods, fires, droughts, famines and diseases in just the first fifteen years of the seventh millennium. The good news is: Jesus is coming soon.

Chapter Eight

The One Less Traveled By

In a newspaper, there was a cartoon of a mother and her young son in their kitchen. A television was on in the kitchen, and it showed a huge asteroid on a collision course with the earth, and in the background, nuclear missiles were being fired. The news reporter said,

"This could be the end of the world", and the little boy asked his mother, "Do I have to go to school today"?

Horatio Spafford was a successful lawyer in Chicago. He had invested heavily in property that was destroyed by the 1871 Great Chicago Fire. The fire ruined him financially, and he was hurt even more by a bad economy in 1873.

He planned to sail to Europe with his family, but he was detained by business. He sent his family ahead. Their ship sank after it collided with another ship, and all four of his daughters died.

When Horatio sailed to meet his wife, and he passed the area where his daughters died, he wrote the hymn, "It Is Well with My Soul". Eventually the Spafford's went to Palestine, and started a group called "The American Colony". With their works of charity, they gained the trust of the Jewish, Muslim and Christian communities. After World War I, they played an even greater role in their charitable works. Their colony became the subject of "Jerusalem", which won a Nobel Prize for author, Selma Lagerlof.

Jesus told us to be innocent like little children. No matter what comes their way, children "bounce back". The teachings of Jesus inspire men and women to bounce back. Whether we face unemployment; disease; a lost loved one or the end of days, God wants us to trust in him.

In general, there are two paths in life; the easy one and the more difficult one. Native Americans taught their children to take the more difficult, upward path; not the easy downward path. Jesus said, "Enter through the narrow gate. For wide is the gate and broad is the road that leads to destruction and many enter through it". (Matthew 7:13- NIV) Jesus Christ is known as the straight and narrow way. Jesus said that He is the way to eternal life.

The great, American poet, Robert Frost, put it well in this excerpt from his famous poem, "The Road Not Taken":

> "Two roads diverged in a yellow wood
> And sorry I could not travel both...
> I shall be telling this with a sigh
> Somewhere ages and ages hence:
> Two roads diverged in a wood, and I –
> I took the one less traveled by,
> And that has made all the difference".

No matter what the circumstances in life, it is the path we take and our faith and disposition that counts. The concern is not when or how soon the apocalypse is coming, but the path we are on. Is it well with our soul? Are we part of the greed, pride, lust and anxiety in the world, or do we practice the peace of God in our lives and with others?

The world doesn't like truth, but we need truth in our lives and our work. Truth in science and religion is more prevalent than most avenues of society. Wouldn't it be nice if the car salesman, the attorney, the politician and the stock broker practiced truth in their professions? The nightly news reports would be a lot more calming if people practiced truth in their lives and professions. Jesus Christ said, "I am the way, and the truth and the life". (John 14:6 NIV)

Is there really truth in life? Is Jesus Christ really the truth? Is the Bible, including the Old and New Testaments, truthful? The author has witnessed many people the last fifty years proclaiming the truth of Christ, and coming to follow the truth of Christ; the path of truth. Truth makes all the difference.

The truth and authenticity of the Bible has made all the difference for millions and millions. In Chapter Two we looked at truth in science. If the medical profession in the late 1700s had observed the truth of the Old Testament scripture, "life is in the blood", it would have literally saved the life of our country's founding father, George Washington.

On December 12, 1799, George Washington was supervising tree work in a wooded are at his Mount Vernon home. In the afternoon, Washington got very wet and chilled from the weather, but being very disciplined, Washington continued to work in his wet clothes. The next morning, he went out to work again. Three inches of snow fell and he got wet once again. He began complaining of a sore throat. Modern physicians suspect that he got strep throat. Today physicians would have prescribed an antibiotic, which obviously, was not available in Washington's day. (from the "Constitution Daily")

Washington gargled with some molasses, vinegar and water, and breathed the steam from vinegar and water. By the evening of the 14th, his overseer was called in to perform bloodletting. His physician was then called on, and he and two other physicians during the next eight hours drained blood from Washington. Thirty-two ounces of blood were drained by the third physician during the final bleeding. It is estimated that half of Washington's blood was drained during the eight hours. (The average body has ten pints of blood.)

George Washington, founding father, first President and great American hero, died from shock on December 14,

1799, at age 67. As in Washington's day, even a majority of doctors and scientists can be set in their ways. Leaders in any field can make wrong decisions, including in religion and in science. Yet, the Holy Bibles' authors claim that the scriptures were not inspired by man but by God, "For prophecy never had its origin in the human will, but prophets, though human, spoke from God as they were carried along by the Holy Spirit". (2 Peter 1:21 NIV)

One of the greatest tours in the world that proves the authenticity of the Bible is "Ink and Blood" by curator, Dr. William H. Noah. The author was fortunate to tour the exhibit at the Knoxville Museum of Art in 2005. It's very interesting that in the gospel of John 1:1, Jesus is referred to as "the Word". Christians, the largest group of people in the world today, believe in the authenticity of the Bible.

Only God could have an accurate book, of history, theology, and "reality" records of people's personal lives that were recorded over 1,400 years. The author will quote himself from a paper he wrote at Muncie Central in April of 1968 in 12th grade English class, "It is self-evident that a book which can be written by forty authors over 1,400 years must be a complete hoax or a profound revelation as the religious contend".

Skeptics have continued to fail time after time in their efforts to discredit the Bible. A few months ago (early fall of 2015), a news reporter interviewed a young woman in America, and she told the reporter that she didn't believe in the holocaust or in history. For some unexplained reason, she believed that events like the holocaust were made up for some kind of propaganda. It's not surprising that we hear nonsensical comments like this from some in the millennial generation, if we keep in mind what is happening on some of the college campuses. There are many examples of college campuses "gone wild", but it was reported after we rang in

2016, that some campuses are creating safe zones for students who are too immature and too sensitive to understand truth.

Ten years ago, I would have had a problem believing this kind of report, but with all of the irrational thinking on many campuses today, I know the reports are true. It may be hard to believe, but some of the "safe zone" rooms have videos of pets frolicking with each other and coloring books for the students to color in. It reminds me of my kindergarten days, when we got out a mat for naptime. The Israelis have a good practice of requiring service in the armed services after high school. Many of our high school graduates need a touch of reality. If a high school graduate in America served two years, the country could give them veteran health benefits. If the graduate served four years, they could be given a nice G.I. educational grant, as well as veteran health benefits. If high school graduates served in the armed forces immediately after high school, there wouldn't be so many immature and overly sensitive students in college.

Biblical critics for generations didn't have much better ground to stand on than the young woman, who didn't believe in the World War II Holocaust. For generations, skeptics didn't even believe in a King David or the Biblical story of David. In 1993-94, a piece of basalt was discovered in Tel Dan in northern Israel. The inscription on the basalt was in Aramaic. The King of Damascus recorded "the king of Israel" and his alliance to the king of the "House of David". The artifact was proved to be genuine, and today it can be observed at the Israel Museum in Jerusalem.

Some Biblical critics have trouble finding their great grandparent's picture on a genealogy website, but they are bewildered to learn that a picture of Jehu, the King of Israel was found from 841 BC! At that time Nimrud (now Kalhu in modern day Iraq), was the capitol of the ancient Assyrian Empire. In 1846, archaeologist, Henry Layard, discovered one of the greatest archeological finds of all time in Kalhu. It was a 7-foot-tall, black limestone obelisk that had five panels of writing and pictures on its four sides.

The obelisk was made as a tribute to King Shalmaneser III. The five panels on the four sides, show five kings who paid homage and tribute to the King of Assyria. The obelisk was made around 841 BC, during the reign of King Jehu of Israel. He was the tenth king of Israel, after Jeroboam, son of Solomon. The second panel from the top of the sculpture shows King Jehu. The cuneiform text on the obelisk says, "The tribute of Jehu, son of Omri: I received from him silver, gold, a golden bowl, a golden vase with pointed bottom, golden tumblers, golden buckets, tin, a staff for a king and spears".

The obelisk shows the first picture of an ancient Biblical figure, and the only known picture of a Hebrew King (a replica can be seen at Harvard's Semitic museum in Cambridge, Massachusetts). It's also incredible that King Jehu, who is not only shown and referenced on the obelisk, but he also had a big impact on Jezebel and her son, King Jehoram (2 Kings 9-10). Ahab and Jezebel are familiar names to any Bible student. Also, many people not familiar with the Bible as well as some nationally known musicians know that Jezebel is associated with deceit and wickedness.

In 1951, pop singer, Frankie Lane, sang a song entitled "Jezebel", that became a hit. Sade had the song, Jezebel, on her 1985 album. 10,000 Maniacs recorded a song called "Jezebel" on their 1992 album. Kelly Clarkson also mentioned Jezebel on her 2015 album. Songwriters as well as singers might want to include the great prophet, Elijah, in their songs about Jezebel, because Elijah was Jezebel's greatest foe. Elijah even prophesied that Jezebel would be eaten by dogs.

Ahab and Jezebel are a big part of one of Israel's darkest spiritual periods. Ahab was the seventh king of Israel after Jeroboam. He married Jezebel, the daughter of a Phoenician King from the area of Tyre, just north of Israel. Ahab had continued the tradition of worshipping Yahweh, the God of Israel, until he married Jezebel. Jezebel worshipped two pagan gods, including Baal, and she influenced Ahab to turn from Yahweh. Ahab even built her a palace with the idol of Baal as well stocking it with priests and prophets of Baal. Jezebel had many of the prophets of Yahweh put to death.

Elijah confronted Ahab and Jezebel and challenged them with a showdown of the prophet of God against the prophets of Baal. The showdown took place on Mt. Carmel, which is north of the Jezreel Valley, not far from the ancient city of Jezreel. Whoever called down fire from heaven to consume their animal sacrifice on their altar would be the winner. (The record of Ahab and Jezebel is found in 1 Kings and 2 Kings.)

The prophets of Baal built their altar and Elijah built his altar. The prophets of Baal went first and they failed. Elijah then had his altar, wood and animal sacrifice soaked with water, and he prayed to God (Yahweh) in heaven, and his sacrifice was consumed with fire. The crowd then killed the prophets of Baal. Word got to Jezebel, and she was outraged and threatened to kill Elijah.

The last, great notorious act by Jezebel was giving false accusations against a man, Naboth, who owned a very nice vineyard in Jezreel.

Naboth wouldn't trade or sell his vineyard, because it had been in his family for many generations. Ahab was very disappointed, so Jezebel accused Naboth of blasphemy and had him stoned, so Ahab could get the vineyard to add to his gardens. After the stoning of Naboth, Elijah paid Ahab a visit.

Elijah wasn't in a friendly mood, and he prophesied in front of King Ahab that he and his heirs would be destroyed and that dogs would eat Jezebel. Several years later Ahab was killed by a Syrian army, and ten years after that we find King Jehu back at the ranch.

Before we go back to the ranch to catch up with King Jehu, a couple of very significant events happened in the meantime. It was time for Elijah to meet God, and he was taken to heaven in a chariot of fire. Elisha was his worthy successor. Elijah was living, when Ahab was killed, but during the time of Jezebel's demise, Elisha was the main prophet of Israel.

Elisha was told by God to go into a meeting where Jehu was with his military friends. At that time, Ahab's second son, Jehoram was king of Israel (Ahab's first son while king of Israel died from an accident). Jehu followed Elisha out of the meeting, and Elisha anointed him with oil to be king of Israel. Jehu rushed back into the meeting with his friends and made the announcement. Jehu was recognized as king of Israel, and Jehu immediately went to kill King Jehoram.

Jezebel got word that Jehu was now king, and she fixed herself up to look out of the palace tower as King Jehu entered the city. Jehu saw her, and had her eunuchs throw her out of the window. When she hit the ground her blood splattered on the horses and on the wall. Jehu's horse trampled over her, and Jehu went out to dinner. While at dinner, Jehu told some men to go bury her, because she was a king's daughter. When they arrived at her body, all they found were her skull, hands and feet. Wild dogs had eaten the rest of her.

It's absolutely remarkable that the Assyrian obelisk shows the picture and account of King Jehu. It is as equally as remarkable that many of the events involving Ahab, Jezebel, Elijah and Jehu occurred at the valley of Jezreel, that is also called Armageddon. Not only did Naboth, the vineyard owner, live in the city of Jezreel, but Elijah defeated the prophets of Baal on the north side of the valley, on Mt. Carmel. Sometimes when you read the Bible and research the events, it's like a true to life, Sherlock Holmes' case unfolding.

Not only did the Apostle Peter record that the holy scriptures are inspired by God, but the Apostle Paul also recorded in 2 Timothy 3:16 that "all scripture is given by inspiration of God". These claims and facts are important in understanding the prophetic reliability of books of the Bible like Revelation, Matthew, Luke, 1 Thessalonians, Isaiah, Jeremiah, Ezekiel, Daniel and many others.

Both the Apostles Peter and Paul were part of the many prophecies found in the Bible. Peter and Paul were two of the greatest, early Christian leaders. Even though Christ is the cornerstone of the church, Peter and Paul have significant roles. In architecture the cornerstone is the reference stone for laying all the other stones. The other two major stones are the keystone and the capstone. They keep the whole structure together. Christ is certainly the cornerstone of the Christian faith and church, but the Apostles Peter and Paul are the keystone and the capstone of the spiritual temple that God planned for his people.

The author believes that those who believe the ancient temple of God will be built for the third time before the last days could be making a major mistake. Jesus refers to the body as the temple of God. He explains that the church is made up of different parts of the body. In other words, each member of the church is a certain part of the body; who has specific jobs and talents to make up the whole temple or body of the church.

If the Old Testaments and New Testaments are taken into context, we understand the difference of the physical Temple in the Old Testament and the spiritual Temple in the New Testament. This change from the physical Temple to the spiritual Temple runs parallel with the change of God's chosen nation, Israel, in the Old Testament to God's chosen people in the New Testament. In the Old Testament we find a record of the Hebrews being the chosen people of God. In the New Testament we find record of the Gentiles (everyone else) and the Jews being called to serve God.

The determining factor is those who now follow Christ, and the determining factor before Christ's ministry were those who followed the Judaic Law. Those who followed the Law before Christ were the ones who followed God. Many Hebrews or Jews were not in God's will. Today, it's the same principle. Those in God's will today are those who follow Christ and do His will; not those who just have a certain church membership. Like the old preachers use to say: just because you're in the garage, doesn't make you a car.

If one takes the New Testament in context with the Old Testament, the new temple are those who make up the bride of Christ, the church. It has nothing doing with men's names for any of the churches; including Roman Catholic,

Lutheran, United Methodist, Baptist and the other church organizations. God is rebuilding the new, spiritual temple. God's glory use to dwell in a physical temple that was in Jerusalem. God, by the Holy Spirit, now dwells in the members of the new temple or body, which makes up the church. Jesus referred to the true members of the church as "the bride of Christ". God is getting the bride of Christ ready for the last days. Jesus said to be prepared. Don't wait on the rebuilding of a physical temple: Jesus said that he is coming like a thief in the night. The events of the rapture, tribulation and second coming of Christ are coming very soon.

Peter and Paul played very significant roles in the early church. Paul was the greatest evangelist who ever lived. He did more for early church planting than anyone. Peter is also just as significant, if not more so. Peter ministered with Christ for three years. There is more about Peter in the four gospels, than any of the other eleven apostles. Peter was singled out by Jesus a number of times. Peter also witnessed Christ's resurrection from the grave (Mary Magdalene was the other early witness of the resurrection). Peter witnessed the resurrected Christ, and Christ's ascension into heaven. He also witnessed the outpouring of the Holy Spirit on the day of Pentecost. Peter was the featured speaker on the day of Pentecost. Peter also witnessed Elijah and Moses talking to Christ on the Mount of Transfiguration, and Peter along with James and John heard God say at the mount, "this is my beloved Son, in whom I'm well pleased; listen to Him".

The Bible is as authentic as any accurate record of man. It is not just a human document. Even though it defies the cynic's logic, it is inspired by God. Many times it has been documented that Bibles without fire proof containers were the only thing to survive fires. The finding of the Dead Seas Scrolls in the Qumran Caves of ancient Israel further proves the accuracy of the Bible (800 ancient fragments of the Bible were found including part of Isaiah; they were dated to be 100 to 300 years before Christ). The book of Isaiah includes the prophecy that the Messiah would be born of a virgin.

The Bible is the bestselling book in America. The most valuable book in the world is the first book printed on the Guttenberg Printing Press, the Holy Bible! In the last 2,000 years some very significant people have seen that the Bible has kept its accuracy. King Constantine in 331 AD made sure with the finest scholars of his time, that the holy scriptures were accurately translated. Others who safe-guarded the accuracy of the scriptures were Jerome in 404 AD; Steven Langton, the author of the Magna Carta in the 12th century; John Wycliffe in the 14th Century; William Tyndale in 1526 and Martin Luther in 1534. These were just a few of the people who have kept the scriptures accurate with the original Hebrew, Aramaic and Greek languages.

The world is full of cynics; skeptics who stand for nothing. It's easy to be skeptical; it takes no talent or conviction. Anyone could be skeptical about anything at any time. It takes an honest man or woman to take a stand of faith and knowledge for their convictions. People who stand for nothing have been described since the beginning of the scriptures, including Cain; people of Noah's time; Pharaohs who forced the Israelites into labor; Canaanite Kings and tribes, Ahab and Jezebel and many others.

Also, in the New Testament, the Apostle Paul prophesies about the people in the last days in 1 Timothy 4:1-3 (NIV), "The Spirit clearly says that in later times some will abandon the faith and follow deceiving spirits and things taught be demons. Such teachings come through hypocritical liars, whose consciences have been seared as with a hot iron. They forbid people to marry, and order them to abstain from certain foods, which God created to be received with thanksgiving. For everything God created is good, and nothing is to be rejected". "Things taught by demons" are strong words. Today we hear about "being politically correct", but we don't hear about "being theologically correct", which is also a very significant problem.

Modern day psychologists and theologians, don't consider the scriptures or the activities of Jesus Christ, when it comes to the subject of demons. It's interesting that television and movies producers are all over the dark side of demons, including zombies, vampires, witches, ghosts and other "creatures of the night". At the same time, psychologists and theologians ignore the teachings of the scriptures about demons. They also ignore that casting out of demons was one of Christ's main ministries including healing, prayer and teaching.

The Lord's Prayer that Christ taught us (Matthew 6:9-13) does not say "deliver us from evil", but the scripture says, "deliver us from the evil one". Is this just coincidence that most churches don't quote the Lord's prayer accurately? I doubt it. Most churches today practice and preach the social gospel. It's about appealing to the crowd, instead of preaching all of the scriptures; "the whole truth". They avoid teaching and preaching about demons, Satan, hell, sin and anything that might be "insensitive" to the crowd. No wonder that many college students today are too sensitive to hear the truth.

As a former pastor, I've had personal experience with some in the church hierarchy saying that it would be best not to preach about hell. The scriptures, of course, have an answer for this situation as well. Paul, the prophet, also addresses this in 2 Timothy 4:3-5 (NIV), "For the time will come when men will not put up with sound doctrine. Instead to suit their own desires, they will gather around a great number of teachers to say what their itching ears want to hear. They will turn their ears away from the truth and turn aside to myths. But keep your head in all situations, endure hardship, do the work of an evangelist"...

The author went to college during the hippie days, the late sixties and early seventies. It's hard to think of anything good about the hippie movement, but there was a lot of good sounding music at the time, even though some of the lyrics tried to portray their message. Today in the media archives, it's described as a time of "free love". Not so, there wasn't much love about it. There were a lot of arrogant, angry people who enjoyed drugs and promiscuity. So was there any harm in it?

If you were on campus in those days, you would have experienced that the old pin up gals like Rita Hayworth from our parent's generation were replaced by new, full nude pin up gals. The truth is that

Playboy, Penthouse, Playgirl and Hustler of that time, as well as the new X rated movies and the XXX pornography became the precursors of the R rated movies, pornography business and the pornography websites of the later 20th century and early 21st century.

If God was angry in Noah's day, do you think he is angry today? Most of the church crowd doesn't hear about his anger or judgments; it's just about love and peace, like the hippies claimed. God is a God of love, and the two greatest commandments are about loving God and loving one another, but most people don't stop and think about what the scriptures say in the light of Noah's day and today. Logically, if we are in the last days, and if it's like the days of Noah, then God is angry with the wickedness. Unfortunately, most people don't want to talk about the wickedness, they think the word, "sin" is not "theologically correct".

Jesus, the Son of God, was also a great teacher and prophet. He mentioned the last days a number of times, and he talked about hell more than anyone in the scriptures. It's wonderful that many Native Americans have become

Christian. The way of Christ is a great blessing, but like their ancestors, Jesus Christ also talked about the straight, narrow and "upward" path. Jesus clung to the accuracy of the scriptures. We would be stupid not to.

In the Old Testament book of Proverbs 14:12 (English Standard Version), the author wrote, "There is a way that seems right to a man, but its end is the way to death". One of the greatest Christian authors in modern times was C.S. Lewis. He said something very insightful that we will also look at in the next chapter, "Pride leads to every other vice. It is the complete anti-God state of mind". Pride is the downfall of mankind, and in the last days, there is an abundance of "anti-God" activity.

When we apply for a job, we give references. When we apply to enter the halls of higher education, we give references. When we apply for a loan or to purchase a large ticket item, we give references. We have plenty of references from the Bible; from the science of archeology; from historians and from millions of personal, spiritual experiences confirming the authenticity of the Bible. It's worthwhile to look at references also from two very intelligent men, who did prolific work on law and on justice.

Jeremy Bentham was an English jurist. He recorded, "All the massing bulk of our English and American law may be reduced to a very few grand principles underlying the whole and which were enunciated by Moses". If you studied law, you know about Jeremy Bentham. Most of us haven't studied law, but we know who Thomas Jefferson is. Many Americans would claim that Washington and Jefferson are two of our greatest founding fathers. Jefferson was a genius who led our country as the author of the Declaration of Independence and as our third president.

There is a debate among some conservatives and liberals that Jefferson said, "The Bible makes the best people in the world". Some people today even contribute the saying to George Washington. In our political scene today, we here about "fact check". I always liked that well known phrase from the old Dragnet televisions episodes, "just the facts, ma'am". So, let's look at the facts from the "Thomas Jefferson Encyclopedia" (courtesy of the Thomas Jefferson Foundation). Daniel Webster, outstanding senator, statesman and lawyer, wrote a letter in 1852 that quoted what Jefferson had told him. Webster wrote that Jefferson told me, "I have always said, and always will say, that the studious perusal of the sacred volume will make better citizens, better fathers, and better husbands". This letter also appeared in print in 1858. Jefferson's recommendation of the Bible for America and for its citizens should encourage a lot of soul-searching.

Chapter Nine

Adam, Eve and Advanced Biology

It's recorded in Genesis 5:5 that Adam lived 930 years. We don't know how long Eve lived. We do know that Noah was a direct descendant of Adam and his son, Seth. Another descendant of Adam was Enoch, Noah's great grandfather. The only other person besides Elijah, who didn't die before going to heaven, was Enoch. Genesis 5:24 (NIV) says, "Enoch walked with God; then he was no more, because God took him away". God had not planned death for mankind. God has always planned for man and woman to live forever, but God requires obedience, and He hates wickedness.

Can you imagine a disobedient child saying, "I love my dad and mom, and they love me? Even though they love me, I'm going to do what I want to do". Today there are many wonderful churches from different Christian affiliations, but there are also many people in the churches who think like the disobedient child. They know that God loves and forgives, but they continue to think, "I'm going to do what I want to do".

To prepare his followers for the last days, Jesus warned them to watch and pray. The acts of watching and praying include the disposition of faithfulness and obedience. There is no safe haven for disobedience, pride, rebellion and wickedness in the lives of those who are looking for the soon coming of Jesus Christ.

God required man to work. God never indicated that it was alright for man to not work. God never sent Adam checks or stamps. Genesis 2:15 (NIV) says, "The Lord God took the man and put him in the Garden of Eden to work it and take care of it". We find out early on that God is also a God of judgment. He also told Adam that he must not eat from the tree of the knowledge of good and evil. God told Adam that he would die, if he ate from it.

The warning of death for man first appears in Genesis 2:17. Millenniums later, God is still warning man of not only death, but eternal separation in hell, if he does not follow the commandments of Christ. Jesus said in John 14:21 (NIV), "Whoever has my commandments and keeps them is the one who loves me. The one who loves me will be loved by my Father, and I too will love them and show myself to them". We can rightly conclude that based on this scripture and many parallel scriptures that Jesus Christ will not show himself to those who don't keep his commandments. Like many of Christ's teachings on hell, John 15 also teaches eternal separation. For centuries people have wondered, if Adam and Eve are in heaven. I would like to think that after their disobedience, and after being thrown out of the Garden of Eden, they would have been repentant and followed God. Many people today wonder if they will have a second chance to make heaven, if they're not taken in the rapture. The book of Revelation is very clear about a second chance, but it's not a pretty picture.

Let's imagine that the rapture just took place, and a close family member or friend disappeared with millions of others. The person left behind knows some scripture and is somewhat familiar with the rapture, and he or she feels for sure that the rapture took place. Revelation tells us that those who are left and refuse to take the mark of the beast will be executed, but they will be with God.

The problem today is the same problem that Adam and Eve had; most people want to do things their way. It may be their attitude in church, because they think they know best. It might be that a person doesn't go to church, because once again, they think they know best. I shared the gospel of Christ with one person, who said that he learned how to worship from his dad. He said that his dad taught him that he could worship God anywhere. While church services are being conducted, they could go fishing and supposedly worship God. In this case, being half wrong is being "dead" wrong. It's true that we can worship God anywhere, but if a person doesn't serve God, the old preacher says that the devil is stokin' the fire for them.

Isis members think they're taking a quick path to heaven, but Satan has deceived them by taking them on a quick ride to hell. God sent His Son that all might come to the knowledge of the truth, but unfortunately, most don't. We all hope that family members and other loved ones learn to follow Christ. Why don't most people follow Christ? Why were there so many wicked people in the world during Noah's time, that made God think about destroying mankind?

Let's look again at the statement by C.S. Lewis from the last chapter. Lewis' quote applies to Adam and Eve, Cain and every person who wants to do it their way. Lewis said, "Pride leads to every other vice. It is the complete anti-God state of mind". Satan became "anti-God", because of pride and rebellion. Adam and Eve were kicked out of the Garden, because of pride and rebellion. Satan lied to himself; to Adam and Eve and still lies to mankind today. Current politicians would deny that they're not anti-God, but look how they lie and belittle opponents to get elected. Satan tells the world that lies are credible. Many of the millennial generation think that it's alright to cheat and lie. Why wouldn't they, if they're listening to the news, and getting their ideas from the world?

Adam and Eve were tempted, but we're all tempted. They disobeyed God, because of pride; they thought they knew best. Things changed drastically after they were kicked out of the Garden. Things always go downhill, when we disobey God. Who today would have the courage to say that America and its economy are going downhill, because most of our politicians and citizens do not obey God.

There is one question that no skeptic has been able to answer logically about Adam and Eve. Scripture tells us that Adam (and mankind) was made in the image of God. Adam was made not to die, but to live forever. Since Adam was to live for eternity, why is it unbelievable that he lived for just 930 years? Adam was physiologically made, literally, to live forever.

Non-skeptics agree that man was made to live forever and that man use to live longer. Besides Elijah and Enoch, who were taken to heaven without experiencing death, there were about five hundred people who witnessed seeing the resurrected Christ. The original disciples also saw Jesus ascend into heaven. No one is sure how Moses was taken to heaven. We know that God did not allow him to go into the land of Canaan. We don't know if he was directly taken to heaven or taken after death. We can feel assured that it was time for him to move on.

The Apostle Paul recorded that the Spirit took him to the "third" heaven, which he saw, but God did not allow him to describe it. We hear about many people near death who see Jesus; a loved one; brilliant light; or heaven. Some people, even days before they pass on, claim that they have been visited by relatives or other loved ones. As a pastor, I've been with many people, as they have passed on. One parishioner was a shut-in, but he was a very astute person during that time. He was a veteran of the Battle of the Bulge and very bright. I thought a lot of him as a man of God. He had an accident one evening, and I met him and his wife at the emergency room. That night he had to be transferred to a larger hospital.

I slept at home that night, but continued to pray for him. I didn't realize that he was passing on, while I prayed. During that time, I had a very realistic dream in which I saw him. At that time, he was about ninety, but in the dream he looked 35 to 40. In the dream, it was a perfect day at a big country estate. The home had a large, beautiful lawn and a very large front porch. A lot of people were talking on the lawn, and I could see my friend on the steps of the front porch. After I woke up, I found out that he had passed on.

We know that people die, because Adam and Eve disobeyed God. To us, it may seem like a severe punishment, but not really; Adam and Eve had it made, and God warned them of the consequences of disobeying him. Skeptics today, also think that they know best; and they're still following in the steps of Adam and Eve.

Followers of Christ understand why every man and woman has an appointment with death. Billy Graham said that he's not afraid of death, but it's the dying part that bothers him. We're all human. Who wants to take that last breath? There is a bright side to death. For the followers of Christ, it's a great homecoming! C.S. Lewis said, "Death is a new beginning". This life is a journey, and the after death experience is a greater and infinite journey! The prophet Isaiah gives us words of assurance in Isaiah, chapter 43, "Fear not, for I am with you".

What changed in Adam's and Eve's bodies from being immortal to lasting about 900 years? Also, what changed in the bodies of Adam and Eve to the children of Abraham, where man went from 900 years to living under 120 years? At creation, God breathed the breath of life into man. Is there a spark from God in man and woman that diminishes from infinity to hundreds of years to less than a hundred years? The answer may lie in discoveries made in the fields of advanced biology and physiology.

For many decades there has been a shallow report that the cells of the human body renew themselves every seven years. Like with so many simplistic reports, only a portion of the statement is true. It is true that most of the cells in the body replace themselves every seven to ten years, and there are from 50 to 75 trillion cells in the human body!

Based on scientific research, it is possible that the cerebral cortex in the human brain is the receiving end of God's spark! The cells in the cerebral cortex are never replaced. If a cerebral cortex neuron dies, it is not replaced. The cerebral cortex cells are very different than most of the cells in the body. Most of the cells in that part of our brain are with us until death. The general make-up of man lies in the cerebral cortex. The attributes of memory, consciousness, language, perception, attention and thought come from the cerebral cortex.

Another part of the body that could be affected by the "spark" of God is the heart. The cells in the heart do not regenerate like most parts of the body. The regeneration rate is only about 1% of the heart cells per year. By age seventy, the rate of regeneration is cut in half. Many of our heart cells are original from birth, when we die.

The scientific minded are more likely than most theologians to observe the connection between the created, immortal man to the mortal man, who is promised eternity through Christ. Christians understand that man is created in the image of God, but man and woman went their own way by disobeying God. Of course, they paid the price by becoming mortal; again by the hand of God. As God breathed the breath of life into man, He also renews life in man and woman through Christ. The book of Revelation says that "only those whose names are written in the Lamb's book of life, will be with God in his "holy city". (Revelation 21:22-27 NIV). This passage also says in verse 21 that there was no temple, because "the Lord God Almighty and the Lamb (Christ) are the temple".

In any age, apocalyptic or non-apocalyptic, followers of Christ have an innate desire to share Christ with others. I grew up with two very intelligent guys, my brother, Dr. Richard Clark and my first cousin, Dr. Thomas Sills. Like my brother and cousin, I was also interested in science at any early age. In ninth grade, biology was my favorite subject, and in 10th grade, zoology was my favorite subject. In ninth grade, I entered the regional science fair at Ball State University, while my cousin, who was in 12th grade entered the same fair. I received an honorable mention, and my cousin won first place at the regional science fair, which allowed him to go to the national science fair!

Through the years I shared my thoughts about Christ and the Bible with my brother and cousin. My brother received his doctorate in medicine from the University of Rochester, and my cousin received his doctorate in physics from Purdue University. I continued to talk to my brother about Christ during the period that he received specialties in internal medicine, allergy, dermatology and bio-engineering. I also continued to share the gospel with my cousin, as he continued to teach physics at a college in Chicago.

As I alluded to in the forward, I was amazed that my brother also believes that we are close to the apocalyptic age. As a scientist, he sees from mathematics and science what Christ prophesied about in Matthew 24: the last days. The last, longer conversation I had with my cousin was after he wrote the book, "What Einstein Did Not See" (by Thomas W. Sills, Dearborn Resources-Chicago-2009). I'm not a student of physics, but I learned the significance of his book from a remarkable review on Amazon: "This may be the most important Physics book ever written...Sills takes us from Einstein's non Euclidean Space, replacing Einstein's time dimension with Sill's "time space" ... With Sill's new formulation, Physics will go as far beyond Einstein as Einstein went beyond Newton" .... (Amazon Customer on September 16, 2012)

In chapter six, we looked briefly at time travel and the fourth dimension while sharing the UFO sighting. Even though I was only twenty-three at the time, I believed in the fourth dimension many years before I turned twenty-three. Allow me to blow one more mental fuse in you, by referring to the "New Jerusalem" as recorded in Revelation 21. The New Jerusalem comes on the scene after the last days and the final war at Armageddon. The author can't say that the city is fourth dimensional, but it does defy gravity. The city is as high as it is long and wide! (It's a good thing that the scriptures say that the redeemed will be like angels!)

The city will be as wide as roughly, one third of the United States, and it will be as long as one third of the United States, and it will be as high as one third of the United States! I think the creator of "The Jetsons" had the same concept in mind. The New Jerusalem will be a larger living area than anywhere in the world, because it is as high as it is wide and long. The width and length would be almost the distance from New York City to St. Louis, Missouri, and the length would be almost the distance from Chicago to Tallahassee, Florida. Just imagine it being that high as well!

The more we think about the reality of the description from Revelation 21, and concepts from scientists like Einstein and Thomas Sills, and the thousands of documented UFO sightings, the more we get a grasp of what heaven is like as well as the fourth dimension! There are one of two last steps for the people now living on earth, either the rapture or the tribulation, which is the apocalypse.

People can speculate and say that if it hadn't been for Adam and Eve's rebellious spirit, their billions of descendants would not have had to go through all of the suffering and waiting. Allow me to blow just a small mental fuse in you; God is omniscient (Omni-science!). Since God is all knowing, He would have known about Adam and Eve's fall from grace before He created them! In seeing the future, God is like a million Nostradamus's and Edgar Cayces rolled into one being. God is also like one gigantic world-wide computer that sees all things and knows all things from the past, present and future!

Because of God's omniscience, we can be assured that God has always had a definitive plan. Whether God wanted a huge population of perfect, immortal people in the Garden of Eden, or a huge population of saints in heaven, God is in control. There is more than enough room for billions of Adams and Eves in heaven!

The record accuracy of the first couple, Adam and Eve, is important to help confirm the Genesis story, as well as the whole of the Bible. Modern science also confirms the accuracy of the Adam and Eve story. Geneticist, Dr. Nathaniel Jeanson, has traced DNA to one couple. As Jeanson focused his research on DNA, he found that mankind can trace their beginning to a common man and woman. Jeanson's work has centered on the Y chromosome, as well as the DNA from the mitochondria, that is in the cells of the egg.

Eventually, scientific research, archeology and the Biblical account will lead the skeptic, as well as the non-skeptic to decide for themselves. Either Biblical accounts, including the accounts of Adam and Eve and the accounts of Jesus Christ, are reality or myth. The existence of God is either reality or myth, and the existence of heaven and hell are either realty or myth.

Jesus Christ had a continual problem with the Pharisees and the other teachers in the temple. They seemed to discard the truth for political reasons. Does that sound familiar today in our society? Even though the Jews believed in the coming of the Messiah, most of the Jewish leadership and educated members of their society did not recognize Jesus as the Messiah, the Son of God. On more than a couple occasions, Jesus called the Pharisees and other teachers hypocrites.

Why is it that skeptics would rather doubt a modern miracle; one in the Bible or a Biblical account like Adam and Eve in the Garden of Eden, than exercise a logical mind and look at all the evidence that corroborates the Bible? Are they also hypocrites, because they criticize those who stand for the truth, while they stand for nothing? One thing that the hypocrite cannot deny is the toxic world that we live. One of the great proofs of needing God is the way mankind has ruined the earth. We started in the Garden of Eden, and now we live in a toxic world; something has to give.

It's very sad what has happened to Detroit and other cities. It is not only the toxic environment, but also, the loss of manufacturing plants and jobs. Many other towns have also been hit by the loss of manufacturers, like my hometown, Muncie, Indiana. Even though industry was still strong in Muncie in the sixties and seventies, my hometown began to lose industrial jobs in the sixties, when Ball Corporation (Ball Brothers at that time), moved most of their manufacturing to another state. After the eighties, Muncie lost all of their major manufacturers, including Chevrolet, Delco, Borg-Warner (originally Warner Gear) and Westinghouse.

Over five years ago, I went by Chevrolet, where my dad retired, and it looked like a war zone. The huge plant and nice office building were torn down, and no building left standing. In some of the parking lots, large pieces of concrete were torn up.

When I was a kid, my family and I would go through Detroit to see my uncle and his family in Royal Oak. Detroit is not the city that it uses to be, but the same is true with other cities as well as small towns. I read "Dynamics of Small Town Ministry" by Lawrence Farris. He accurately describes the dynamics of four different types of small towns and their evolution. Earlier I shared how Native Americans have had reservation land taken away and/or devalued by the building of prisons; landfills and dams. The same thing has happened to some of our smallest towns. The end result is almost a ghost town. Small towns also become smaller, if they are not near a bigger town or if they lose their main employer.

The experience of lost jobs, environmental compromises, and safety in cities and towns is depressing. At this time (January, 2016), Flint, Michigan, is struggling significantly, because of lead getting in their water supply. Also, the stock market is taking a nose dive. On December 31, 2015, the Dow Jones average was 17,823. Twenty days later, the Dow jones Average was 15,628.

Some financial advisors/investors are saying that like Greece, the United States is becoming the next, great debtor nation. As this book goes to the publisher, our country will be at an indebtedness of 19 trillion dollars. It's almost impossible to comprehend the huge debt, but if the government wants to add something to their budget, they just add the cost to the debt and print more paper money! Interest costs on the debt for 2016 will be more money than the total budgeted for education, transportation and general government expenses.

One could say that mankind is going full circle from the Garden of Eden. The Garden of Eden was plentiful; the world now is filled with hunger. The Garden of Eden was peaceful; the world now is filled with hate and violence. The Garden of Eden was safe; the world now is unsafe. The Garden of Eden was healthful; the world is now full of toxins. As we approach the apocalypse, it is essential that we follow Christ, if we want to experience the full circle, and return to the new Garden of Eden: The New Jerusalem.

God wants man and woman to abide with him in peace and happiness. Even in a toxic world, mankind can still be close to God. Christ told us to follow his commandments, if we love him. God not only wants to give us love now, but also a better life. He wants us to love others and to be healthy.

We do have a health challenge, since the world is full of toxins. Canada has about 35,000 chemicals in commercial use. The United States has about 70,000 chemicals in commercial use. In our bodies, lead, cadmium, mercury, and arsenic are the most common heavy metals that cause us problems. Aluminum is another toxic problem in our bodies. There are about twenty-three toxins that cause us the most health problems, but many people have about 130 foreign chemicals in their bodies as well. Flame Retardant, a PBDE chemical, is in 90 to 97% of the American population. PBDE chemicals are linked to delays in physical and mental development; memory and thyroid problems; reduced fertility and lower IQ. Some flame retardants are linked to cancer.

Mercury is one of the most severe heavy metals that is poisoning bodies. It is the cause of many health problems, including Alzheimer's and Parkinson's Diseases. Mercury in general causes damage to the brain, kidneys and lungs. With all of the problems that Mercury causes, there are still three other severe heavy metals: arsenic, cadmium and lead. In addition, aluminum and eighteen other heavy metals are poisonous to the human body. If that is not enough, in many people medical scientists find dozens of other foreign chemicals.

Fortunately, if someone gets sick from these toxins, biochemists and other researchers have invented drugs; some are safer than others. The greatest news are antioxidants that God has created in food groups like dates, strawberries, blueberries, green tea, acai and many others. The body is also cleansed when foods are excreted. Deep breathing also helps remove toxins. Today, natural chelators for cleansing the body have been improved on. Chelation therapy is also available.

God given intelligence provides mankind with healthy remedies. Like learning God's will, healthful practices have to be sought out. We will never be in the original Garden of Eden again, but until we go full circle to the New Jerusalem, God has provided healthful foods and remedies for us. Even though we live in a toxic world, there is healthy living available to part of the world. Even though we live in a sinful world, there is freedom in Christ available to everyone!

The Bible claims that the first man is Adam, and there is now genetic proof that the human race came from one couple! Just don't try to prove that you came from Adam and Eve through Ancestry.com! Adam's existence is further bolstered by references to Adam in the Bible, outside the book of Genesis. There are four references to Adam in the Old Testament (outside of Genesis), which are Deuteronomy 32:8; Joshua 3:16; 1 Chronicles 1:1; and Job 31:33. There are also seven references to Adam in the New Testament, including Luke 3:38; Roman 5:14; 1 Corinthians 15:22,45; 1 Timothy 2:13,14 and Jude 1:14.

Not only do we have eleven references to Adam outside of the book of Genesis, but the first five chapters of the Bible contain a lot about Adam. References to Adam that go back in history from over 2,000 - 3,000 years ago do not likely point to a person of mythology. Some people read so much about Greek mythology that they get Zeus mixed up with Yahweh, and Hermes (Mercury in Roman mythology) with Gabriel. The case for the reality of Adam and Eve is much stronger than the skeptic realizes.

Many people agree that everything is cyclic: the weather, the economy, the seasons, rain to evaporation, photosynthesis to oxygen, and of course, the Garden of Eden to the New Jerusalem! It's also very interesting that the Bible virtually begins with the Garden of Eden and virtually ends with the New Jerusalem. Of course the Bible begins with Genesis 1:1, "In the beginning God created the heaven and the earth". Already in Genesis 2:7, we find Adam, then the Garden of Eden in Genesis 2:8! The Bible ends with Revelation 22:21, "The grace of our Lord Jesus be with God's people. Amen". We find New Jerusalem described in Revelation 21! From the beginning of the Bible, there are 38 verses before the Garden of Eden is mentioned, and the New Jerusalem is mention 46 verses before the end of the Bible!

Is it coincidental? Many time Jesus answered a question with a question. Let me ask: is it coincidental that Isaiah prophesied that the Messiah would be born a virgin seven hundred years before Jesus was born? Was it coincidental that Jesus prophesied to the disciples that He would die for the sins of the world, and rise again on the third day? The inspired words of God are not coincidental. God has always had a plan for mankind, and for every one individually. God had a plan for Adam and Eve in the Garden of Eden, and he also had an advanced plan for billions of men, women and children in the New Jerusalem!

The journey in this life is what counts for each individual; the upward path, that narrow way in Jesus Christ. As we walk with Christ on our journey, we don't have to worry about the benefits; they're built into the eternal policy. The Garden of Eden was a given for Adam and Eve, and the New Jerusalem is a given for those who walk with Christ. We are direct descendants of Adam and Eve through Noah!

Some people ask about where the different races came from. The beauty of the answer is that it doesn't matter! Some Bible scholars and historians say that the different races came from Noah's three sons: Ham, Shem and Japheth. There's not a lot of logic to those theories, because the three sons of Noah had the same parents, and they were similar in DNA! The one type of evolution is within species. A bird's tail feathers can grow longer. A polar bear is white in the Arctic instead of brown or black. In the human race there are more than three races or three colors like brown, black and white. When I think about environmental changes within the human species, I think of red heads and blondes coming from northern Europe and darker skinned people coming from warmer climates.

In the Bible, God and his prophets didn't warn about different races marrying; they warned about marrying outside the faith! Solomon and the nation of Israel got into big time trouble, because Solomon married foreign wives of different, pagan beliefs, and Solomon appeased his pagan wives with places and temples for them to worship their pagan gods. One of my favorite Bible teachers is Steve Brown of Key Life Ministries. I started listening to Steve when cassette tapes were the latest technology!

One of my favorite sayings of Steve's is how he distinctly defines the human race into one of two categories: "believers or pagans"! Even in the time of the Israelites, the same was true: believers or pagans! If someone tries to tell you differently, borrow another one of Steve's favorite sayings: "it smells like smoke"!

All of us have one of two destinies. If we follow Christ, it is the destiny of the believer to be with Christ in the New Jerusalem. If we follow the broad way of the pagan, it is the destiny of the other place that smells like smoke! Are we really that much advanced of Adam and Eve? Not that much, mostly we are more advanced in time and inventions of technology. We are more ways alike than different. We are created in the image of God. When we walk with God, we're doing well. When we don't walk with God, it can be a big problem. Adam and Eve were from the Garden of Eden, and the believer is headed to the New Jerusalem. I personally believe that Adam and Eve, like Moses and Elijah, will be with the believers in the New Jerusalem. Why would one believe that about Adam and Eve? Because, they were saved by God's grace!

The human race, in particularly the believer, is connected with Adam and Eve in the Garden of Eden, as we approach the apocalypse; preparing for the New Jerusalem. We are going full circle: from the Garden to sin, and from sin to the New Jerusalem, through Christ, God's grace. The believer has the fiery trial of life and death to walk through, as we prepare. Many believers, like Enoch and Elijah, will never know death. They will be raptured as the world walks into the apocalypse.

Adam and Eve experienced a new beginning after they were expelled from the Garden. They felt the pangs of sin, but they survived and were nourished by God's grace. We were born into sin, but we will survive and be nourished as we feed on God's Word and walk with Christ. The Garden of Eden was paradise, and some wonder how Adam and Eve could lose paradise. Remember God's plan and omniscience. He has us covered by Christ, and He knows all things. It was tough when mankind was kicked out of the Garden, but it is absolutely wonderful that God is ushering us into His kingdom.

Chapter Ten

The Good, the Bad and the Prophets

What matters this moment, as the apocalypse approaches, is your place in life and what the prophets say. The Bible says that a "good man" is full of faith and the Holy Spirit. To put it simply, be on the side of good by following the commands of Christ. The other place is the broad way that incurs the wrath of God. Any terrorist or people who sponsor terrorism; any humanist who prefers man's logic over God's will; any skeptic of Christ and His purpose are all anti-God. Like the Anti-Christ, they are the opposite of what God intended for mankind. The follower of Christ is God's perfect will; the opposite of the counterfeit in society. What the prophets of God say about the last days is also of great importance.

Spiritually, mankind is still building the Tower of Babel, and God is getting ready to tear it down. The mother city of Babylon, Nimrod, was the site of the Tower of Babel. Babel and several prophecies of Babylon in the Bible lead us to the approaching apocalypse. One is a prophecy that comes to the Prophet Daniel to interpret a dream of Nebuchadnezzar's, King of Babylon. (Daniel 4:23-27 NIV) Daniel told Nebuchadnezzar that he would be driven away to the wilderness, and live with animals and eat grass like cattle. Daniel continued to prophesy to King Nebuchadnezzar, "your kingdom will be restored to you when you acknowledge that Heaven rules". One year later the prophecy was fulfilled. Nebuchadnezzar's kingdom was restored, when he yielded to

God. He said, "Now, I, Nebuchadnezzar, praise and exalt and glorify the King of Heaven".... (Daniel 4:34-37 NIV)

There are three Babel and Babylonian events and prophecies that tie into a related prophecy in Revelation. First of all, after Belshazzar replaced his father, Nebuchadnezzar, as king Babylon, two very significant prophecies were fulfilled: the destruction of Belshazzar and the destruction of Babylon as an empire.

In Daniel chapter 5, we find Belshazzar throwing a big pagan party with drinking and a big feast. As Belshazzar, his wives, his concubines and his nobles drank from the goblets of gold from the temple of God in Jerusalem, you might say that another Tower of Babel experience was about to happen. (Daniel 5:1-30) All of a sudden God showed up in the form of a human hand writing on the walls. Belshazzar's face turned pale and his legs gave way. The king's astrologers and other spiritualists could not interpret the writing on the wall.

Daniel interprets the dream and basically tells Belshazzar that you are proud of your paganism, but "you do not honor the God who holds in his hand your life and all your ways". Of course, the same state of mind exists in most people today whether their paganism involves skepticism, humanism, atheism, communism, terrorism, sports, entertainment, pleasures or anything else worldly that is cherished above honoring God.

The very night that God wrote, "Mene, Mene, Tekel, Parsin" on the wall, Belshazzar was killed. "Mene" means that God brought his reign to an end; "Tekel" means that Belshazzar was "weighed in the balance and found wanting" (King James Version), and "Parsin" means that Babylonia is now given to the Medes and the Persians. Darius, the Mede took over the kingdom. Babylon was vanquished, and the Medes and Persians took over the empire. Darius was the son of Xerxes. Cyrus, Kind of Persia, replaced Darius. Under King

Cyrus, the Israelites were freed, and allowed to return to Jerusalem and their homeland.

God is a God of deliverance. He always sets his people free. He saved Adam and Eve after their fall in the Garden of Eden. He saved humanity with Noah and the ark. He saved Jacob and his sons, the early Israelites, from famine through Joseph in Egypt. He saved the Israelites from Egyptian bondage through Moses. He saved the Israelites from their bondage in Babylonia. He saves "whosoever will" through His son, Jesus Christ. He is also getting ready to save His people from the approaching apocalypse and destruction. The author had the privilege as a young evangelist in the mid-seventies to minister in a Persian church in Chicago. I had an interpreter as I ministered and gave the message. Speaking of God's deliverance, in that service, we witnessed the healing of a crippled person.

The Tower of Babel; the rise and fall of Babylon and the Babylonian figure in Revelation 17:5, "Babylon The Great, The Mother of Prostitutes and of the Abominations of the Earth", all tie into the current spiritual, Babylon, and its destruction at the end of the apocalypse. The current, spiritual Tower of Babel or Babylon, is all the carnality or anti-God element in the world. The old saying applies, "you're either for me or against me". Anything that is not godly is carnal. Anything carnal is the spiritual Babylon or Tower of Babel. The great harlot or "Babylon the Great" of Revelation is Apostle John's definition of the modern, spiritual Babylon. The spirit of Babylon and rebellion will be destroyed when Christ returns during the Battle of Armageddon.

Just like the roots of Ginseng confirming what the plant is, the roots of the original Babylon (Nimrod) confirm what Babylon is. One of Noah's three sons, Ham, was the father of Canaan. (Genesis 9) Ham disrespected his father, and Noah said, "Curse be Canaan"! The lowest of slaves will he be to his brothers". Ham's son was Cush, and Cush's son was Nimrod, a great leader and hunter. Nimrod started several villages that became cities. Nimrod also started the city that was named after him, and Nimrod later became the center of Babylon. After the flood God told Noah and his sons to spread out over the earth and multiply. But Nimrod remained in the original area of the ark, and many people hunkered down there as well. The Bible says in Genesis 11:4 that the people wanted to "make a name for themselves" and they built the tower. God confused their language; the building stopped and they were scattered over "the face of the whole earth". (Genesis 11:9)

God will soon stop the world. The spiritual activity of rebellion, pride and greed will stop, when God intercedes to stop the carnality, the spiritual Babylon. The prophecy in Revelation 17 concerns an apocalyptic event that is near the end of the world, as we know it. It sounds like God is getting ready to punish the nations of the world for their evil. The Apostle John describes a figure that is called "Babylon the Great", who many call the Great Harlot. Revelation 17:18 describes the harlot of Babylon: "The woman you saw is the great city that rules over the kings of the earth". The other figure mentioned in this chapter is the Beast, that represents kings and nations.

Some scholars say that the Great Harlot represents Rome. They are probably partially right, but when the reader takes the Babylonian Harlot in context with the Beast and the rest of the chapter, it appears that the Harlot and the Beast are representing the carnality or sins of past and current nations. Babylon and Rome were two ancient, pagan empires, but today, many nations are serving paganism and the ways of man, instead of the ways of God.

Revelation 18 clearly sums up what the Great Harlot stands for. Revelation 18 basically describes that the Spirit of Babylon or Babylon the Great has made the kings (leaders) of the earth and the merchants of the earth drunk with her carnality, "the wine of her adulteries". (Revelation 18:1-3 NIV) Once God deals with the spirit of Babylon, the people who follow the riches and other carnalities of Babylon are in mourning. The world, its armies and leaders, are very upset with losing their "spiritual leader". Revelation 19 and the beginning of Revelation 20 talk about their destruction.

In the book of Revelation, God reveals how much he hates the wickedness of mankind. He hated it when Adam and Eve fell from grace; he hated it before the flood and he still hates it. The "social gospel" or soft-pedaling the gospel is misleading, because God hates sin. Yahweh, the creator and God of love, is also a jealous God and a God of judgment. It's unfortunate that many churches have turned a deaf ear to the true nature of God. The social gospel churches do not want to hear the truth that God hates wickedness. God has judged mankind before, and He will judge mankind as the apocalypse unfolds.

Discussing the judgments of God is something like discussing a bear market; it's not pleasant. A bear market is a reality when it happens, and the apocalypse of God's judgments will be a reality. No one in their right mind wants a bad economy, and no one wants to experience the apocalypse, but it's coming. Jesus and prophets of the Bible warns us of the apocalyptic events of the end time; as well as secular prophets like Nostradamus.

In Chapter 11, we'll look at God's power, and his power of deliverance. In Chapter 12, we'll look at His kingdom, and how we can avoid the apocalypse. You might say that Chapter 12 is the ultimate, prepper's chapter. The apocalypse is not a pretty picture. Beginning in Revelation 6, things get downright scary. God has some messengers and angels that will deliver a smack down that makes the WWE look like a Sunday School picnic. Isis will wish that they had never been born, when God begins to unleash his wrath with his messenger angels.

The middle of Revelation can be depressing. It could be really hard to take, if it weren't for the end of Revelation. The current chapter of this book could be hard to take, if it weren't for the next chapter. The follower of Christ can always look ahead and see the silver lining, when they're in a storm.

It's good to keep in mind what Helen Keller said when she was introduced to Jesus Christ. She said, "I knew him, I knew him; I just didn't know his name!" If you don't know his name, it's excellent advice to get acquainted. Don't wait; start now! If you do know his name, get as close to him as possible. You need him every day, and He wants you to be close to him every moment of your life.

I'm glad that I've known him through many, many experiences in life, and I'm sure glad that I know him, when I get to Revelation 6! Christ has more for us than the Pale Horse and the rider called, Death and Hades. (Revelation 6:8 NIV) Between Revelation 6 and Revelation 16, it seems like one third of the earth was destroyed, then one third of what was left was destroyed, then another one third was destroyed of what was left again. Well, that has to be an overstatement, but let's look at what does happen during the apocalypse.

In Revelation 6, a rider on a fiery red horse was given power to take peace away from earth, "and make men slay each other". Continuing in the sixth chapter, a pale horse with Death and Hades as the rider has power over one fourth of the earth to "kill by sword, famine and plague, and by the wild beasts of the earth". In the end of chapter six, the leaders of the earth announce the apocalypse. A sixth seal was opened, and a great earthquake moved the mountains and the islands. The rich and the leaders of the earth hide in caves and announce: "For the great day of their wrath has come and who can stand?" (Revelation 6:17 NIV)

The apocalypse is now in full swing, and announced by the pagan, worldly leaders. Revelation 7:9-17 gives us a wonderful break, and virtually announces that the many people who were not raptured, and followed Christ after they were given a second chance, do not have to go through the rest of the "great tribulation" (the apocalyptic events). (This will be looked at more thoroughly in Chapters 11 and 12,) Verse 9 describes, "a great multitude that no one could count, from every nation, tribe, people and language, standing before the throne and in front of the Lamb (Christ). An elder in this chapter asks who all of the people are, and he is answered with, "These are they who have come out of the great tribulation". We know that they are the followers of Christ, because the passage says, "they have washed their robes, and made them white in the blood of the Lamb". (Revelation 7:14 NIV)

Meanwhile, we return to the apocalypse in Revelation 8. When the seventh seal is opened, we find seven angels with seven trumpets. The destruction of earth continues as the first angel sounds his trumpet. With hail and fire from heaven, one third of the earth is scorched. The second angel announces what appears to be a meteor that lands in the sea. A third of the sea is "turned into blood, a third of the living creatures in the sea died, and a third of the ships were destroyed". (Revelation 8:8,9 NIV)

After the meteor falls, it is possible that "a great star" is an asteroid that falls next. In verse 10, the prophecy of John describes, "a great star, blazing like a torch, fell from the sky"... According to the number of apocalyptic prophecies in Revelation, it looks like the world is in the middle part of the tribulation by chapter 9. The really scary part of the apocalyptic tribulation begins in chapter 9. In verses 2-11, John describes a lot of horrific locusts that come out of hell with a sting like a scorpion. As the passage continues, it is like an Edgar Allen Poe horror show. Verse 7 says that the locusts "look like horses prepared for battle", and that their faces look like human faces. The passage continues to tell us that they have teeth like lion's teeth. It says that there is a king over them, and he is "the angel of the abyss ... whose name is ... Apollyon" (Satan).

Revelation 10:11 is a very significant prophecy verification: "Then I (the Apostle John) was told, "You must prophesy again about many peoples, nations, languages and kings". Basically, God is telling John, the Apostle of love, that you are my end time prophet to tell nations, people and world leaders about the end of days as man knows them (the apocalypse). Skeptics need to hold on to their seats now, because in Revelation 11:15, the seventh angel announces the meaning of the apocalypse: "there were loud voices in heaven, which said: The kingdom of the world has become the kingdom of our Lord and of his Christ, and he will reign for ever and ever". This announcement says it all: The Kingdom of the World has become the Kingdom of Christ"!

I feel sorry for those who believe in an apocalypse, but they don't know the purpose of the apocalypse. The apocalypse will not destroy the entire earth by an earthquake, nuclear warfare or asteroid, but prophesied apocalyptic events will happen, because God is taking over the world! The last verse of chapter 11 in Revelation gives proof that the rebuilding of the physical temple in Jerusalem is not necessary for the return of the Messiah. Revelation 11:19 says, "Then God's temple in heaven was opened, and within his temple was seen the ark of his covenant. And there came flashes of lightning, rumblings, peals of thunder, an earthquake and a great hailstorm". What an announcement of God's Temple returning to earth!

Beginning in Revelation 11, the followers of Christ can be in celebration mode. God is in the process of establishing his kingdom on earth! It's very possible that most of chapters 13 and 14 are out of chronological order with Revelation 7:9-

17. In Revelation 7, we find that repentant people during the first part of the tribulation are taken out of the world (by execution), and saved by God. These are the people who refuse to take the mark of the Beast. Many of them probably understood what had happened at the very beginning of the tribulation, when many millions of people (the church) were raptured.

Revelation 13 describes the beast, and the mark of the beast, 666. The last part of chapter 14 describes the harvest of the earth. It's important to look at Revelation 14:13, because it explains the multitude that we find in Revelation 7. Verse 13 says, "Then I heard a voice from heaven say, "Write: Blessed are the dead who die in the Lord from now on. Yes, says the Spirit, they will rest from their labor, for their deed will follow them".

Information in Revelation 15 about seven angels and seven plagues prepares the reader for information in chapter 16. Revelation 16 is a very eventful chapter, and loaded with information. Most importantly, God announces the end of the apocalypse (the great tribulation)! Revelation 16, verse 17 (NIV) says, "It is done!" The seven angels with the seven bowls of God's wrath are before verse 18. They are punishing the people who took the mark of the beast; the pagans. As the bowls are dished out by the seven angels, there are painful boils; blood that makes everything in the sea die; blood in rivers and springs; fire that scorches people; darkness with pains and sores; and three evil spirits that come out of the beast, false prophet and dragon.

The last verse of Revelation 16 is a very unusual and shocking account of a hailstorm. Verse 21 says, "From the sky huge hailstones of about a hundred pounds each fell upon men". Falling hail that is five to ten pounds each would cause a lot of damage to humans, deer and other mammals. But hail that is a hundred pounds each would kill a grizzly bear, lion and an elephant. Imagine the damage it would do to vehicles, buildings and other structures!

The two most important events for the follower of Christ in Revelation 16 are the announcement of the end of the tribulation, and the confirmation about the last great event at Armageddon. Verse 14 confirms that the last apocalyptic event is called, "the great day of God Almighty". Verse 16 confirms that the location of this last, great battle is at Armageddon (the Valley of Jezreel). The three evil spirits mentioned in Revelation 16:13 and 14, gather the evil forces throughout the world to fight the followers of God at Armageddon. Besides Chapters 11 and 12 of this book being on the Kingdom of God and "ultimate preppers" chapters, we will also look at John's prophecies in chapters 19-21 of Revelation.

The anti-God theme runs throughout chapters 6 to 18 in Revelation. The anti-Christ, the Beast, the False Prophet, the Dragon and Babylon the Great (the Great Harlot) are part of Satan's anti-God team. Even after billions of pagans go through the tribulation, their hearts are still wicked. Revelation 16:11 says "they refused to repent of what they had done". Revelation 16:21 says, "they cursed God "...

Many people today put the things of the world first. Christ has to come first (His way or the highway)! As I write this, the first 2016 primary in Iowa is just two days away. We hope the weather is not severe, because a large snow storm is arriving in Iowa on Monday night (February 1). It seems like a lot of the candidates resort to tactics that are unbecoming of those who follow Christ. There are some candidates who are Christian, and there are other candidates that would say anything to win the election. One candidate in particular is known for being dishonest, and the country doesn't need a dishonest president in 2017. Particularly, in chapter two we looked at the importance of expounding the truth.

In 2006, the comic strip "Non Sequitur" did a good job of describing the world's perspective of truth today. It's a skit about "Noah's Publisher". A publisher is interviewing Noah about sharing his experience, and the reader assumes that the publisher knows that the world is going to have a hard time accepting Noah's story of the flood and ark. The publisher says to Noah, "No, I'm not asking you to lie. I'm asking you to embellish the truth for the sake of marketing". The comic strip is a great commentary on how "the world turns".

The spread of the Sahara Desert to its south is a reminder of how the ways of the world spreads into the hearts and minds of mankind. The Sahara is spreading southward at a rate of thirty miles a year. It's affecting a lot of countries including Senegal, Mali, Niger, Chad and Sudan. There are so many factors affecting the health and economy of nations across the world.

The Sahara is also in Egypt, which is at the foot of the Middle East. Some political and sociological analysts are saying that the Middle East could be the fuse and the center of World War III. The Saudis are against Iran, and Iran seems to be against almost everyone except terrorists. Like Iran, terrorists seem to be against almost everyone except Iran. There is a lot of turmoil between the tribes of the Middle- East, and almost everyone in the Middle-East is against Israel.

It is comforting to know that God has a specific plan. No matter how many conflicts are escalating across the world and at home, God knows exactly the direction we're headed. The way that God leads the followers of Christ is good news for the believers. No matter how abrasive the 2016 primaries and election are, God is in control. During the current administration, it is hard to understand why American leaders are allowing our country to decline.

Israel has been one of our closest allies, but the current president is more concerned about appeasing Iran than being a staunch ally of Israel. The current administration is diminishing our military. The Marines have two thirds of the battalion as normal. The Air Force has the oldest and smallest combat aircraft in history. The Navy is also smaller, and it cannot meet potential security demands. The manpower in the Army is ten percent smaller. The Army's forces are being shrunk to a pre-World War II level. In 1940, the U.S. population was 132 million. Today (by the end of 2015), the U.S. population is 322 million. The pre-World War II population was 41% of what it is today! In other worlds, the population today is 2.4 times as great as in 1940. Can you believe that a United States administration would let our military diminish to 1940 levels? Former Secretary of Defense, Chuck Hagel, said the current military "might not be able to respond to multiple conflicts".

If one follows the trail of all the defense secretaries that the current president has had, one can understand the dissatisfaction with this president. There have been four defense secretaries in less than six years under the current president: Bob Gates, Leon Panetta, Chuck Hagel and Ashton Carter. In eight years, George Bush had two defense secretaries. Ronald Reagan also had two defense secretaries in eight years. Both defense secretaries, Bob Gates and Leon Panetta, criticized the current, controversial president for "centralizing power and micro- managing security policy and decisions". Defense Secretary, Chuck Hagel, resigned at the end of November, 2014. After Hagel's disappointment of serving under the current president, he advised the next defense secretary to "listen to the military". One could assume he was also saying to listen to the military more than to the president.

I've heard many evangelicals say that they feel the 2008 and 2012 elections were judgments of God on America. In 2012, former presidential supporters were saying the same, as well as voicing their disappointments in the "hope and change" propaganda. The author is a great believer in constitutional government, especially freedom of speech and religion. Everyone has a different opinion like the church committee members picking the color and style of carpet. Tolerance of speech and religion is admirable and patriotic. Not everyone believes that the mainstream media pulled the wool over the public's eye in 2008 and 2012, but many do. More and more people are becoming aware of the political bias in the mainstream media.

Prayer for America is crucial. While weakening the military, the current White House administration has hurt our relationship with many allies; Israel is at the top of the list. Israel is the nation of spiritual heritage for Jews and Christians, Catholic and Protestant. Our alliance with Israel needs to be greatly strengthened again. It's a hard line to say that any of Israel's enemies are anti-God. Terrorists and nations that sponsor terrorists have the evil traits that qualify them as anti-God.

Prayer is needed for our allies. The current administration has let them down in Europe, the Middle East and in Asia. Russia has interfered in the affairs of Ukraine, and many people have been killed. Russia is taking advantage of the situation. The United States said they would build a missile defense system in Poland, but this administration reneged. Russia is also extending its power in the Black Sea, while taking advantage of a weak United States administration.

In the Middle East, America has let down Israel, Jordan and Syria. America has not aggressively taken the fight to Isis. The current president has a weak reaction policy, rather than a strong action policy The "Iran Deal" has hurt many allies, especially the Middle East allies. From just one deal, the president and secretary of state appear to be out of their minds. Iran is totally taking advantage of the current administration.

America's alliance with Japan had better be solid, because China is aggressively encroaching on several countries by usurping territorial waters. In the South China Sea, China has made islands equipped with airfields, ports and lighthouses by expanding in waters that are close to the Philippines, Brunei, Malaysia and Viet Nam. China has expanded hundreds of miles to the south and to the east in territorial waters. Look at a current events map, and see how close China has Encroached upon these Asian countries.

Like the old western movies and episodes (Rifleman is one of my favorites), there was always the bad guy and the good guy. In real life, globally and locally, it seems like there is usually the bad group and the good group. It is real life: the broad way and the narrow way. The anti-God group is alive and well. It is up to the people of strong character and faith to stand for what is right.

Roman 14:23 (NIV) says, "whatever is not of faith is sin". About twenty years ago, a friend of mine took her daughter on a cruise in the Caribbean. A hurricane blew in so the captain went back around the island to avoid the hurricane. Unfortunately, the hurricane turned also. The cruise ship met up with the hurricane, which broke the ship's pool and water supply lines. The food was destroyed, and the passengers and crew had no food or water. They were stranded from the hurricane for over twenty-four hours. My friend said that she thought her daughter and her would die.

God had another plan for them, and my friend told me about the trip, when she returned home. Sometimes we feel that we have seen our darkest hour, or day or year. Even though it can seem that we're at death's door, God has other plans for us. God has eternal plans for us as well. Some of the greatest people have been martyred for the cause of Christ.

It's hard to believe that an established church would keep God's word from the people for over one thousand years.

As late as the early 1500s, William Tyndale lived a personal type of apocalyptic experience for years. He tried to translate the Bible into English for the common person, but he was sought for trumped up charges as a heretic. He had to flee into Germany so he could translate the Bible.

Even in Germany, bishops and spies tried to find him, because he was sending his translated work into England. They wanted to execute him so the Bibles wouldn't get into the hands of the common person. Finally, they found him through spies who pretended to befriend him. They brought him back to England, and burned him at the stake in 1536. He prayed for the king of England, and three years later King Henry VIII ordered that every parish was to have the English Bible. When the King James Bible was translated, they mostly used William Tyndale's work. To this day, the King James Bible and the New International Version are accurate translations from the original Hebrew, Aramaic and Greek.

Prophets, martyrs and scientists have taken a stand for God's Word for centuries. John Napier lived after William Tyndale from 1550 to 1617. He was a very talented scientist, and he invented logarithms. Even though Napier was a genius in physics, astronomy and mathematics, he had an intense interest in the book of Revelation. Napier believed in the Apocalypse, and in 1593, he wrote a book called, "A Plain Discovery of the Whole Revelation of St. John".

It would be an honor to just be in the company of prophets like the Apostle John; Christian scientists like John Napier and Bible scholars like William Tyndale. Those who follow Christ have all the riches in the world. Jesus said, "Do not store up for yourselves treasures on earth...But store up for yourselves treasures in heaven"... (Mt. 6:19,20)

About seven years ago, I was getting ready to start a new pastorate in central Indiana, when I heard that my first cousin by marriage had passed on. He was about four years young than I am, and a dedicated Christian, who helped many. He had fought a long battle with cancer, when God took him home. During the funeral service, my cousin shared how his family was gathered around him right before he passed on. The last thing he said was, "I sent my treasures before me". You could hear a pin drop in the sanctuary. I've served many years in the ministry, and that was one of the best testimonies that I've ever heard or read.

Chapter 11

The Laws of God and Science

Earlier we looked at Isaac Newton as a man dedicated to Christ and science. Isaac Newton discovered the three laws of motion, that are still being used and observed in modern science today (after 329 years). Newton's original publication of the three laws of motion came to print in 1687; in Latin. Newton's third law was originally translated as, "When one body exerts a force on a second body, the second body simultaneously exerts a force equal in magnitude and opposite in direction on the first body". Today we simply describe it as, "For every action, there is an equal and opposite reaction".

In football, a safety running into a wide receiver are both experiencing the impact and the reaction of both bodies of motion. Both vehicles in a head on crash experience both the action of the impact and the reaction to being hit. We don't find a stated physical law in the Bible similar to Newton's third law of motion, but we do find spiritual teachings that are similar to Newton's law. One is the spiritual law of reaping what we sow. Another are the laws of love: we love God because God first loved us. The dramatic similarity is the battle of good and evil that ends in the last apocalyptic disaster: the great day of the Lord Almighty at Armageddon. The Apostle Paul aptly defined the conflict between good and evil in Ephesians 6:12 (NIV), "For our struggle is not against flesh and blood, but against rulers, against the authorities, against the powers of this dark world and against spiritual forces of evil in the heavenly realms".

The pagan or unbeliever does not realize the protection and power that God gives. Sometimes the believer does not realize the extent of God's power and protection. Some people say that everyone has a guardian angel. There are examples of guardian angels in the Bible, and the Bible also describes how angels minister to us. Hebrews 1:14 says. "Are not all angels ministering spirits sent to serve those who will inherit salvation?" Personally, I know that we have guardian angels. I can say for sure that my guardian angel saved me twice from car altercations that otherwise could have resulted in death or serious injury. Another time, neighbors witnessed my youngest son's guardian angel, when a drunk hit him two months before his high school graduation.

Guardian Angel

One Sunday evening I was preaching at my church in Mt. Holly, North Carolina, as a lay minister. As I ministered, I knew most of the faces in the crowd except one. I kept going back to one face that I didn't know, because my spirit was telling me that an angel was listening to me. I tried to tell myself that he was a stranger, but my spirit kept saying he was an angel. I was not able to confirm that he was an angel, because he disappeared from the crowd. What I do know is that my guardian angel kept me safe from two car altercations. In the second altercation, I felt the angel's hand holding up my van, and pointing it in a safe direction.

When I was in college at the age of twenty, a friend in my hometown invited me to his cousin's wedding, which was in the hills of Tennessee (somewhere between Crossville and Jamestown). He drove the whole way from Muncie, Indiana, to Tennessee in his old GTO. I offered to drive, but he said he was fine. We got to their house about 3:00 in the morning. We stepped over sleeping adults downstairs, and upstairs all of the young people were sleeping in one big dormer. We went to the wedding by noon that day.

We headed back to Indiana that afternoon. It was raining, and we were driving around the asphalt curves in the Tennessee mountains. My friend looked like he was tired, so I offered to drive again, and he gave me the wheel. I was use to driving on all kinds of roads in all kinds of weather, but even though I took one curve properly, the car swerved and we were heading for the cliff on our right side. My friend was smaller than average, and he started scooting down under the dash on the floor board. I know that we were both praying. To our surprise the car stopped before it fell off the cliff. My friend and I told each other that we would gently crawl out. When we did, the drop off was below our feet, and the edge of the cliff was in front of us. It was the proverbial cliffhanger.

I don't think that I ever told my mom and dad how close of a call that was. A person would be crazy to say that the power of God or our guardian angels didn't save us and the car. We were close to Albany, Kentucky, so my friend hitched a ride into town, and about an hour or so later, he came back riding in the tow truck. After the car was towed off the edge of the cliff, we were amazed once again that the car wasn't damaged. We hopped in, and drove back to our hometown. After we started back, my friend told me that he forgot to tell me that the torsion bar was broken, and you had to adjust the steering for it!

In 1990, I had just completed a fourteen-hour work day in Charlotte, North Carolina, when I got in my van at 11 pm that evening. I started out to drive to home in Mt. Holly, during a very heavy rain storm. When I got on I-85, a lot of the cars had pulled over. At 55 mph I was passing what cars were left on the road. I had just passed a car, when my van hit a lot of water and hydroplaned. All of a sudden I was going down the interstate backwards at 55 mph! I tried to steer the van back around, but it kept edging off the road to the point that I could feel the van beginning to fall off the road to the right, where there was a steep drop-off.

As soon as I felt the van beginning to roll off the road, I felt something grab the van. The next thing I knew, the van was going down the Little Rock Rd. exit ramp! A power had grabbed the van to keep it from tumbling off the road, and pointed it down that exit ramp. It was like I was part of a model train set-up being controlled by the operator. My van didn't have automatic pilot. Once again, a person would be crazy to say that wasn't my guardian angel.

My youngest son was two months away from high school graduation in 1998, when a drunk hit him. It was a terrifying experience that you hope no one has to go through. He was seriously injured. He and his girlfriend had just returned from a hockey game in Charlotte, and he had just dropped her off. His girlfriend's best friend was the second vehicle on the scene. My mechanic was the third vehicle on the scene. My mechanic friend cut the seat strap off from my son's neck. The drunk did not take the curve and T boned our car.

After my mechanic made sure the ambulance was on its way, he drove two miles to our house and came to my back door. It's a shocking experience for anyone to go through. When I arrived on the scene I saw the rear wheels and the drive shaft sticking out at a 90-degree angle to the front of the car, and the roof was caved in.

I saw my son in the ambulance. One of the ambulance workers said there was a good sign that he had just started talking. After those first 48 crucial hours, my son had improved a lot. The doctor put him in a body brace that he wore for three months. Later the neurosurgeon at the hospital in Charlotte told me that he had three other similar accidents that month. He said that one person died; another became a quadriplegic and the third had a permanent injury for life.

My son was able to finish high school from home, and he went to graduation in a body brace and graduated with honors. About one week after the accident, I talked with one of my neighbors whose daughter was my son's girlfriend's best friend. They told me how their daughter and several people, who were first on the scene, witnessed an angelic experience. They said my son was semi-conscious, when they arrived at the car. He was saying, "Is the blonde-headed lady alright?" My son's girlfriend was a brunette. Her best friend knew that he wasn't talking about his girlfriend and that he had just dropped off his girlfriend. My neighbors said that their daughter and several other people with flashlights were searching for a blonde-headed lady in the field where the car was. His girlfriend's friend realized later that the blond-headed lady was an angel. She talked with his girlfriend later and found out there was no blonde-headed lady in the car with them!

After my son was released from the hospital, I also talked with my mechanic, and thanked him for helping. He said the evening of the accident, he had a strange experience. His girlfriend lived out of town, and he hadn't been back very long from his girlfriend's house. He said that he always makes coffee at home, but for some reason, it came over him that evening to go into town for a cup of coffee. Because of his trip to town, he was the third vehicle at the accident scene! Our car that was crushed and split in half was testimony in itself of God's delivering power through a guardian angel.

There are a lot of Biblical scriptures about angels, and several about guardian angels. One of my favorites is from Psalms 34:7 (KJV), "The angel of the Lord encampeth round about them that fear him, and delivereth them". God delivers His people. In this chapter, we will look at some of his delivering powers, including angels. In chapter 12, we will look at how God will deliver his people from the world and from the apocalypse.

One of the greatest promises in the Bible is found in Revelation 3. God is giving the Apostle John a prophecy for the church with encouragement and promise. John is not only referring to the ancient church that was in Philadelphia, but the church of Philadelphia was also the standard for a faithful, obedient and loving church. Philadelphia was a town in Asia Minor that had a large Greek community. Philadelphia was the "gateway to the east". People in commerce traveled from Rome to the east through Philadelphia, and people from the east traveled through Philadelphia.

Most of the ruins of the ancient city are now covered by a Turkish agricultural town that is covered with grapevines. The big drawbacks to ancient Philadelphia and neighboring towns were the fault line and volcanic activity that were in the vicinity. They caused earthquakes and a lot of damage to cities like Philadelphia.

Two of the great accomplishments of the followers of Christ in Philadelphia is that they kept God's commandments and honored God. (Revelation 3:8-9 NIV) The tenth verse contains a great promise and prophecy, not only for the followers of Christ in Philadelphia, but for the followers of Christ today (the church). Revelation 3:10 says, "Since you have kept my command to endure patiently, I will also keep you from the hour of trial that is going to come upon the whole world to test those who live on the earth".

In Christendom, there is a variety of beliefs about the tribulation (the apocalypse) and the rapture. Some Christians don't believe in a rapture that precedes the coming of Christ at Armageddon. Some of Christ's followers believe that the rapture takes place during the middle part of the seven-year tribulation and many followers believe in the pre-tribulation rapture of the church (Christ's followers).

Revelation 3:10 takes the guess work out of when the rapture takes place. God will keep the followers of Christ "from the hour of trial (the tribulation) that is going to come upon the whole world". Not only will God deliver his followers from the apocalypse, but he also protects his followers on earth with angels. Psalm 91:11 proclaims, "For he will command his angels concerning you to guard you in all your ways". What a great promise of protection! Many families like my own have experienced God's hand of protection by His angels.

Being a follower of Christ is a win/win situation. His followers know about grace, love, forgiveness and deliverance. God looks after his followers on earth, and his followers have the greatest retirement plan on earth and in heaven. After I wrote the last paragraph, I had to check on another win/win situation. A lot of people may not understand why I'm writing this chapter during the 2016 Super Bowl.

I'm in Peyton Manning's corner because he played for Indianapolis in my home state, and because he played at University of Tennessee, where I lived in Knoxville for seven years. I also have an interest in the Carolina Panthers, because I worked in Charlotte and lived in Charlotte and that area for many years. I was a big fan of the Charlotte Hornets, when they came to Charlotte in 1988. I was also a fan of the Carolina Panthers, when they came to Charlotte in 1995.

There is only one winner in the Super Bowl, but there are billions of winners in Christ. It takes conviction, commitment and consistency to be a follower of Christ, and it's the most rewarding life on earth (physically and spiritually). Hebrews 2:7 says that we are made a "little lower than the angels". It's up to us to take advantage of being made in the image of God, and being made a little lower than the angels. Unfortunately, many people do not activate what God has given them. All they have to do is make a call to God in prayer, and activate all the privileges waiting for them through Christ.

If someone freely puts a new car in your drive, and you never open the door and start it up, then you do not take advantage of the privileges waiting for you. If you open the door and get in, you're now in the driver's seat. All you have to do is obey the laws of the road, and you can drive that car for many purposes and missions, as long as you want to.

Revelation 3:20 is a great scripture about our potential relationship in Christ. It says that he is standing at our door, and knocking in hopes that we will open the door. The scripture says that He wants to fellowship with us, and wants us to fellowship with him. As we get to know Him, we learn his ways and commands, so we can always abide with him for now and eternity.

It's very comforting to know that God delivers the follower of Christ and protects the person. It's even more exciting to know the powerful message that Jesus gives his follower in Matthew 5:14 (NIV), "You are the light of the world!" It may be hard to comprehend, but the followers of Christ are the light of the world! The real state of the world and mankind is up to each follower of Christ. If the followers of Christ could comprehend what that means, there would be no depression or anxiety problems among them. There were many times the Apostle Paul had nothing materially, but he said that he was anxious for nothing.

As I write these words, the country is right between the super bowl from last night, and the New Hampshire primary tomorrow. I hate to say this to the football fans, but what matters is not the winners of the super bowl, but what the followers of Christ are doing. They are the light of the world! It doesn't matter who wins the New Hampshire primary, because what matters is the activities of those who are "the light of the world". I wish that I could tell all of the followers of Christ throughout the world how important they are. What the followers of Christ are doing and accomplishing will last for eternity!

The apocalypse (the great tribulation) has to come. It's coming does not depend on the Dow Jones Industrial Average or the amount of the national debt. It's coming is part of God's plan for the earth. His followers will be taken from the earth before the beginning of the great tribulation. Those who know about friends or family that followed Christ, and are no longer with them will understand that the rapture has taken place. Those people have a second chance. If they refuse the mark of the beast, they will be executed, but they will be with God and His followers for eternity.

God wants all to be delivered, but not all will be delivered, because billions in the world are following their own ways, humanism, as well as other pagan ways. It's very important for mankind to understand that the God of love is also a God of judgment, because He hates wickedness. Revelation 6 through 16 is very clear about God's avenging angels during the apocalypse. Psalm 78:49 (NIV) says, "He unleashed against them his hot anger, his wrath, indignation and hostility – a band of destroying angels".

Some would say that this passage is just directed toward the firstborn of Egypt, who were killed, while the Israelites sought their freedom. The passage is also a precursor of God's angelic activities in the apocalypse, as well as a reminder of his wrath during previous eras like the time of the flood. Getting Egypt's attention to let the Israelites go; mankind's attention concerning the flood and getting mankind's attention with inspired prophecies about the apocalypse is God's warning that He will address the struggle of evil and good. Many times at a funeral, I've heard, "He was a good man", or "She was a good woman", but God says that a good man or woman is full of faith and the Holy Spirit.

God tells us many times in scripture that He will take care of wickedness and disobedience. God addressed Adam and Eve's disobedience. Why wouldn't He address mankind's disobedience today? Do people today think they are more important or more special than those at the time of the flood? There is a spiritual warfare as well as physical warfare.

Many today don't acknowledge the power of darkness; a real Satan and real demons. Jesus had a constant struggle with Satan and demons while on earth. He rebuked Satan, and cast many demons out of many people. One day my mother received a call from one of her best friends. She has now passed on to glory, but I will call her Lisa. After Lisa told my mother what was going on in her life, my mother told her that you might want to talk with Billy (what my relatives and childhood friends called me), because he is now working as an evangelist.

I talked on the phone with Lisa, and the following is her true story. Lisa said, "Billy, I don't understand what is going on, but I'm seeing evil looking creatures, when I look outside toward my neighbor's house". I asked her if there was anything different in life. Lisa said, "I'm in a ladies social group, and there is a different person who is a newer member. She says that she is a witch, and she started loaning me books on witchcraft". I said, "First of all, return her books; tell her you're not interested and that you don't want to talk about it anymore". I asked Lisa, if I could come and visit her at her house.

When I arrived at Lisa's house, I asked God to lead me. Lisa invited me in, and we set down and talked. Since Lisa was a very nice person, I thought she might know Christ, but she said that she was not a follower of Christ. I told her that I believed the witch and the demons were trying to influence her. Lisa didn't know Christ and His way, and the witch and demons were taking advantage of her vulnerability.

I told Lisa that we should pray and ask that God deliver her from this demonic influence. I said, "Lisa, would you like to become a follower of Christ, and pray with me?" Lisa said that she wanted to give her life to Christ. Lisa and I prayed the prayer of confession and forgiveness, and she accepted Christ as her savior. After she committed to following Christ, I prayed a prayer of deliverance, and God did deliver her from the witch and the demons. Lisa didn't have any more problems with the witch or with seeing the evil creatures. She followed Christ the rest of her life, and she and her husband became faithful members of my parent's home church.

The powers of darkness are real, and Satan and his demons are real. God's delivering power is real, and God's army is real. Revelation 5:11 (NIV) says, "Then I (the prophet John) looked and heard the voices of many angels, numbering thousands upon thousands, and ten thousand times ten thousand"... Ten million angels is unfathomable power. Even one angel or just a few angels make a lot of havoc. All the population of China, India and the United States is a drop in God's creation compared to the power of just a few angels or a raging river of thousands of angels. The population of these large countries also pale in comparison to all of the saints or followers of Christ who are alive as well as those passed on to glory.

The followers of Christ today should have a real concern for those not following Christ. God didn't spare the people of the world during the flood; only Noah and his family. Also, God did not spare his angelic creation that rebelled against him: including Satan. 2 Peter 2:4-10 (NIV) refers to the rebellious and evil angels that God cast out of heaven; the Apostle Peter wrote, "For if God did not spare angels when they sinned, but sent them to hell...if he did not spare the ancient world...he condemned the cities of Sodom and Gomorrah by burning them to ashes and made them an example of what is going to happen to the ungodly...the Lord knows how to rescue godly men from trials and to hold the unrighteous for the day of judgment".

Peter speaks like Jesus spoke about deliverance, judgment, heaven and hell. God's followers should always be assured that God rescues them. The cynic, the humanists and other pagans should be notified that their time is short. They can also follow Christ and be rescued if they so choose. In my lifetime, the satirists made fun of the image of a man holding a sign that says. "Repent and Be Saved!" The news of the sign is especially bad news for the pagan, but it's also an invitation to the pagan to walk with Christ on the narrow and upward path.

Jesus said, "there is rejoicing in the presence of the angels of God over one sinner who repents". (Luke 15:10 NIV) There is rejoicing over anyone who decides to follow Christ, no matter what their circumstance in life. Christ has every type of member and talent that he needs in his kingdom, and he wants people from every walk of life. Let's look at how important just one of many professions is in the body of Christ.

Scientists who dedicate their life and work to Christ, play a significant role in His kingdom. Scientists are working with God's creation, and giving mankind a better understanding of the universe, the earth and its inhabitants. Many of us are animal lovers. Veterinarians like many others in the health profession are working in God's creation; with animals.

Physics is one of the great sciences, and Newton's laws of motion are the foundation of physics. ("What Einstein Did Not See" – Thomas Sills) It's wonderful that Newton was dedicated to Christ and science, and Einstein understood how religion and science complemented each other (one needs the other).

Scientists and physicists like Newton, Einstein and Sills give us a better understanding of how God's creation works. Of course, there is a lot that they don't know, but they have increased our understanding. I have seen a UFO, and have experienced the work of guardian angels, but there is a lot I don't understand. Newton, Einstein and Sill's works in physics help shed some light on travel in the case of UFOs, and on a different dimensional city, which the New Jerusalem is in vertical space as well as length and width, that we read about in Revelation 21.

Newton's laws of motion; Einstein's theory of relativity and Sill's work on time and motion move us even closer to appreciating the power of God's omniscience and omnipotence. Sill's work helps physicists understand even more with his work on "new four-dimensional, Euclidean physical space". ("What Einstein Did Not See" p.11 Thomas Sills)

Man is little more than scratching the surface in understanding the intricate and vast wonders of God's creation. Physical principles like the laws of motion and spiritual principles like reaping what we sow bring us closer to God. Besides the principles of God and His universe, there are also great promises of God that help us in preparation and understanding.

If someone asked me, "what is one of the most important things I need to understand in preparing for the apocalypse". My answer would be: "have an understanding of the bride of Christ". For a better understanding of how God is preparing the bride of Christ, we'll go to a surprisingly, enlightening Old Testament story.

The book of Ruth tells the story of Naomi, an Israelite who left Bethlehem for Moab with her husband and two sons, because there was famine in their land. Her sons married Moabite women, but later Naomi's husband and sons died. One of the daughter in laws, Ruth, insisted on returning to Bethlehem with Naomi. She told Naomi, "your people will be my people and your God my God". (Ruth 1:16 NIV)

Upon returning to Naomi's home, Ruth and Naomi had very little. They were faithful to God, and their faith was rewarded. They arrived at Bethlehem in time for the barley harvest. (Ruth 1:22 NIV) Ruth went into the fields to pick up (glean) the leftover grain. The field she worked in belonged to Boaz, a relative of Naomi's.

Boaz returned to Bethlehem; asked about Ruth and spoke with her. Boaz asked her to help glean in his field. The second chapter says that Ruth found favor with Boaz. Naomi's husband had land, that Naomi decided to sell. The closest kinsman in those days had first right of refusal. With the purchase of the land, came the obligation of taking care of the widow, Naomi and her daughter-in-law. The closest kinsman redeemer turned down the land, so Boaz, the next closest kinsman redeemer, bought the land and assumed the care of Naomi and Ruth. The greater prize than the land was his right to marry Ruth!

The book of Ruth closes with some very interesting information in chapter four. The genealogy of Kind David is given, and the reader finds out that Boaz and Ruth were David's great grandparents. (Ruth 4:17 NIV) We also know from the Bible that Jesus was in the lineage of David. (Luke 3:31 NIV)

It's remarkable how similar the story of Boaz and Ruth is to Christ (the bridegroom) and the church (the Bride-Christ's followers). There are at least seventeen passages in the Old and New Testaments in eight different books (including Isaiah, Matthew, Ephesians and Revelation) about the bride and bridegroom. In heaven the union between Christ and his bride, the church, is at the marriage supper of the Lamb.

Naomi had a plan for Ruth and Boaz, not unlike God's plan for the church and Christ. Ruth and Boaz met in a field that needed harvesting. It was not coincidence. God prepares his followers to meet with those who have a need. Where do they meet? They meet in a field that needs harvesting. Christ emphasized that the fields are ready for harvest, but the laborers are few.

Ruth made a commitment to Boaz, and they were united as man and wife. The follower of Christ makes a commitment to Christ, and they become the bride and the bridegroom. Boaz became Ruth and Naomi's kinsman redeemer. A redeemer gains possession and compensates for faults. Christ is the redeemer of His followers, because the bride commits their life and soul to Christ the bridegroom, and Christ forgives their faults or sins. The big difference between the union of a man and wife compared to the union of the bridegroom, Christ, and the bride, the church, is the first is temporal and the latter is eternal.

The next and last chapter explains the final preparation for the apocalypse (the great tribulation). It expounds on the bride of Christ and the Kingdom of God. These writings pale in comparison to the most beautiful literature ever written,

Revelation 21 and 22, which explore the final episode for mankind on earth.

Chapter 12

He Is Coming Real Soon

Preparation is a key value in life. We prepare food and an exercise regime to be fit. We prepare for education by learning basic values to be successful in school. We prepare for college and/or work after high school. We prepare financially by working. Unfortunately, many people today skip the spiritual preparation. When I was a child, we also prepared for life spiritually. My family attended church regularly. I learned the Bible by attending classes and by studying. I prayed and gave my life to Christ. It's sad today that many people have not learned the Bible, and they have not learned the ways of Christ.

Commitment is another great asset in life. When I was seven years old, my parents offered to get a used piano and to give me weekly piano lessons, if I promised to practice 30 minutes daily. As a child and teen, I loved playing basketball, but I could not play basketball or do anything else until I practiced on the piano for 30 minutes. I made the commitment to practice daily at the age of seven. I practiced daily for eight years, and God blessed me for making the commitment. Piano was part of my life in church and in school, and I played most of my life, including professionally part-time. I continued to play basketball now and then after college, but playing basketball gradually faded away, but playing piano and teaching others remained in my life.

Discipline is another valuable asset. Reformation founders like Martin Luther and leaders like John Wesley were great examples of discipline. Because John Wesley, the father of Methodism, was so big on discipline, the United Methodist Church today has a standard for the church called, "The Book of Discipline". Discipline can sound scary, but ask any Marine or anyone else that has served in the Armed Forces about the importance of discipline. Millions of Americans today in every type of work and profession know the value of discipline.

The values of preparation, commitment and discipline are greatly needed in many teen and adult lives today. Prayer is needed for discipline, as well as for the future of our country. One good example of a person committed to God and country is former United States Congressman Ron Paul. Dr. Paul was a flight surgeon in the United States Air Force, and later he had a private practice in obstetrics and gynecology. Ron Paul was also a United States Congressman for sixteen years, and he also ran for the presidency of the United States.

Today (February, 2016), Dr. Paul is warning people to be prepared for a change in the currency of the United States. He is promoting Porter Stansberry's teachings on the economy and investing. Everyone should evaluate people's advice on investments as well as everything from good nutrition to proper health care. I have not read Mr. Stansberry's book, but there is information on it at <u>RonPaulMessage55.com</u>

As we hear today about investing in silver and gold, the follower of Christ can't help but remember when John and Peter went to the temple. At the temple gate was a man who had been lame from birth. Peter told him, "Silver and gold have I none, but such as I have given I thee: in the name of Jesus Christ of Nazareth rise up and walk". (Acts 3:6 KJV) Gold and silver are good investments, but they are no comparison to the life invested in Christ. The follower of Christ should always remember Matthew 6:19, 20 (NIV), "Do not store up for yourselves treasures on earth, where moth and rust destroy, and where thieves break in and steal. But store up for yourselves treasures in heaven, where neither moth or rust destroys, and where thieves do not break in and steal".

What is the best investment today? It's Living for Christ! What is the best way to prepare for the apocalypse? Be a follower of Christ! We can't assume that people today know about Christ. I became a casual friend of a lady who worked at a store where I shopped. One day I happened to mention the four gospels. She asked, "what are the gospels?" God gave me the opportunity to share the gospel with her. Like the story of Ruth and Boaz, the fields are ripe for harvest. Unfortunately, laborers are few, and there is not much time left.

I can't disagree with people's interest in material preparation like canned food and silver and gold, but it won't save them from the apocalypse. Only God can deliver us through Christ. The world has turned a deaf hear to the prayer of confession and salvation. We have all sinned. None of us are worthy. God gave us His gift of grace, Jesus Christ. We ask God to forgive us of our sins, and to ask Jesus Christ into our lives. Like Helen Keller said, "I knew him, I knew him, but I didn't know his name".

John, chapter 15, is the Christian living chapter. Whether we go to an independent church, Catholic, Baptist, Pentecostal, Methodist or another denomination, God will not deliver us from the apocalypse, unless we are a follower of Christ. John 15 gives a good understanding about the Christian life. Church attendance and observing rituals won't save us. It's all about our daily relationship with Christ and other followers of Christ. Revelation 3:20 is a great salvation and relationship scripture. Jesus says, "Here I am! I stand at the door and knock. If anyone hears my voice and opens the door, I will come in and eat with him, and he with me". (NIV) Christ is waiting to fellowship with us daily. When we invite him in; follow him daily and fellowship with him and others, we are a follower of Christ. In Joel 2:32 (NIV) God promises that there will be deliverance among the survivors, "And everyone who calls on the name of the Lord will be saved; for on Mount Zion and in Jerusalem there will be deliverance". This prophecy of Joel was proclaimed over 2,500 years ago. The Apostle John expanded on Joel's prophecy almost 2,000 years ago, and about 2,000 years ago Jesus prophesied and taught on the end time. The teachings and prophecies of Christ laid the ground work for Revelation and the days in which we live.

Many of our friends and our enemies believe that the apocalypse is soon approaching. If the beginning of the great tribulation will soon be upon us, then it is urgent that we look at how Christ and His prophets tell us to prepare. It is also necessary to understand that the rapture of the church (the followers of Christ) will take place before the beginning of the of seven-year tribulation. One of the key rapture scriptures was written by the Apostle Paul in 1 Thessalonians 4:16,17 (NIV), "For the Lord himself will come down from heaven, with a loud command, with the voice of the archangel and with the trumpet call of God, and the dead in Christ will rise first. After that, we who are still alive and are left will be caught up together with them in the cloud to meet the Lord in the air. And so we will be with the Lord forever. Therefore, encourage each other with these words". The rapture is a separate event that precedes the return of Christ. Seven years after the rapture, Jesus returns at Armageddon, and defeats his enemies at the Valley of Jezreel and establishes the New Jerusalem.

Jezreel Valley

Jesus also prophesied about the rapture. In Matthew 24:40, 41 (NIV) Jesus said, "Two men will be in the field; one will be taken and the other left. Two women will be grinding with a hand mill; one will be taken and the other left". During the time that I did revival work from Indiana to Texas, one evening I attended a small country church in Missouri. The church was integrated with blacks and whites. The pastor, a former professional heavy weight boxer, said they didn't have a piano player for their praise service. The church didn't have a sound system, so I played the old upright piano extra hard so the people could hear it.

The praise service lasted about two hours. A small, thin elderly man with snow white hair was on the small stage with the pastor. Bless his heart, when he testified he said that the Bible says when the Lord takes the church, two men will be watching TV, and one will be taken and one will be left. I admired that man, because he knew that we had to be prepared. A young attractive woman, who was simply dressed, stood up and sang acapella. She had one of the most beautiful voices that I ever heard. She could have won The Voice or American Idol. She was as good as Whitney Houston. I played those piano keys as hard as I could for the most part of two hours, and after the service I had blood under my finger nails.

The service in that small country church was one of the very best that I've been in. The people loved the Lord; sang His praises and were ready for the rapture. Another rapture teaching and prophecy by Christ is found in Luke 17:30-37. After the rapture prophecy by Christ at the end of Matthew 24, Jesus teaches His followers the parable of the ten virgins in the beginning of Matthew 25. Jesus continues to tell His followers to be prepared and to be ready. He again compares the church and himself to the bride and the bridegroom. He says that five virgins were wise and five were foolish. He says that it took a long time for the bridegroom to come and the five foolish virgins fell asleep. The five wise virgins who were ready went in with Christ to the wedding banquet. The five foolish virgins were shut out. Immediately after the teaching, Jesus warns his followers, "Therefore keep watch, because you do not know the day or the hour". (Matthew 25:13 NIV)

I was getting ready to write about the marriage supper of the lamb, when I took a break to walk and have lunch. As I was finishing lunch, I started to do some channel surfing, when I automatically stopped on Bill Gaither interviewing George Younce. Bear with me a moment while I exercise writer's privilege, and you'll see where this fits into the marriage supper of the lamb. If you haven't followed southern gospel music, Bill Gaither, who is from Alexandria, Indiana (eight miles from my hometown) was interviewing George Younce, probably the most beloved personality in southern gospel music. He lived from 1930 to 2005. Many people know that Bill Gaither has written some of the most popular gospel songs today like "He Touched Me", "Because He Lives" and "The King Is Coming".

As Gaither was finishing the interview, George Younce sang "Suppertime". I had an emotional God moment. I went to hear him and his group, The Cathedral Quartet, in Muncie, Indiana, and later in Charlotte, North Carolina. I've played a lot of kinds of music, and George Younce was my favorite gospel singer, and his group was my favorite southern gospel quartet. As Younce sang, "Suppertime", I was amazed that I already had immediate plans to write about the marriage supper of the lamb. The song typifies the great reunion that Christ will have with his church. The last part of the songs says:

> "Some of the fondest memories of my childhood;
> Were woven around suppertime,
> When my mother used to call
> From the back steps of the old home place:
> Come on home now son it's suppertime.
> Ahhhh, but I'd love to hear that once more,
> But you know for me time has woven the realizations of
> The truth that's even more thrilling and that's when
> The call comes up from the portals of glory
> To come home for its suppertime.
> When all God's children shall gather around the table"...

The marriage supper of the lamb is mentioned in Revelation 19:6-9; right before Christ defeats his enemies at Armageddon. In verse 9 (NIV), "Then the angel said to me, "Write: Blessed are those who are invited to the wedding supper of the Lamb!" It appears that the marriage supper or wedding supper of the Lamb takes place at the time that Christ's enemies are defeated, which is seven years after the church is raptured.

Before the apocalypse begins, Christ warns us many times in all four gospels to watch and pray. He tells us to be prepared and to be on guard. In Luke 21:36 (NIV), Jesus says, "Be always on the watch and pray that you may be able to escape all that is about to happen, and that you may be able to stand before the Son of Man". It would be great that millions of more people would heed this warning and prophecy by the Son of God. The followers of Christ should be diligent to observe this warning by their Messiah.

Return of Christ

Matthew 24:36-44 gives us an idea of the speed and surprise of His coming. It will be business as usual when the rapture takes place. Las Vegas and New Orleans will be partying. Drug addiction will be rampant. Alcohol will be flowing. Isis and those like them will be on the rampage. Wall Street will be investing and selling and trying to get their market share. The news will be brought to the country as usual. But the rapture will take place as in the days of Noah, when all of a sudden the great flood hit the earth.

Many millions, hopefully a billion or more, will be raptured world- wide, and the world will immediately go into chaos. All order in life; segments of families left; great disruption in the economy; many people in government and leadership gone; many talented workers and students will be gone and everything will drastically change.

The earth will go into the apocalypse, the seven years of great tribulation. In verse 42, we are told to "keep watch". Matthew 24:44 (NIV) says, "So you also must be ready, because the Son of Man will come at an hour when you do not expect him". 1 Thessalonians 5:2 (NIV) says that "the day of the Lord will come like a thief in the night". Verse 3 continues with a prophetic warning, "While people are saying "Peace and safety," destruction will come on them suddenly, as labor pains on a pregnant woman, and they will not escape".

Before we look at Revelation 20-22, it is important to understand that the bride of Christ is not certain types of church members. There is no one type of organization or denomination that has special insight into the gospel of Christ. The church of Christ or the bride of Christ is a spiritual bond that is made up of followers of Christ world-wide. They do not fall under a certain realm or group in the world. They are the redeemed who understand scriptures like 1 John 1:9; Ephesians 2:8,9; Revelation 3:20 and chapter 15 of the gospel of John. For a good understanding of who and what a follower of Christ is, read all of the gospel of John. Preparation consists of daily prayer and Bible study in Christ. Read all of the New Testament, then read all of the Old Testament. Develop a close relationship with Christ and other followers of Christ. Share the gospel with people in the world.

Some say that the world is sitting on a time bomb. If that were true, the world would not have survived the black plague over six hundred years ago, and the world would have not survived the potential catastrophes of the cold war in the 1950s and 1960s. God is in control. Sometimes it is hard for mankind to believe that God is in control, but he is. If God weren't in control, mankind would have been destroyed decades ago, since there are so many potential calamities that could cause complete destruction.

God has a plan for mankind. He has one plan for those who follow Christ faithfully, and another plan for those who don't. The Bible is clear about the bride of Christ being raptured before the seven years of the great apocalypse. The other good news is that if a person misses the rapture, and they remember what a friend or relative in Christ shared, they will have a second chance. They will also survive the judgments of God, if they refuse the mark of the beast.

After the rapture of the church and after seven years of tribulation and apocalyptic disasters on earth, Christ will appear over the Valley of Jezreel and defeat His enemies at Armageddon. Revelation 19:11-16 NIV says (through the prophecy of the Apostle John), "I saw heaven standing open and there before me was a white horse whose rider is called Faithful and True (Christ) ...his name is the Word of God (Christ). The armies of heaven were following him... Out of his (Christ) mouth comes a sharp sword with which to strike down the nations...He treads the winepress of the fury of the wrath of God Almighty. On his robe and on his thigh he has this name written: KING OF KINGS AND LORD OF LORDS". And people think that the winners of a super bowl have a celebration!

The rest of Revelation 19 tells that the beast that deceived the world and the false prophet are thrown into the lake of fire. The rest of Christ's enemies are killed by the sharp sword that comes from Christ. The world doesn't understand that Christ has the power to do anything. His designated angels also have power to cause havoc on the world during the apocalypse.

Revelation 20 tells us about the millennial reign of Christ. We have just started out in the seventh millennium, and there is no doubt that the seventh millennium is the millennium of Christ and His church. Even the secular prophet, Nostradamus, said that we are, "Not far from the great age of the Millennium".

In Revelation 20 we find that Satan is bound by an angel of God and thrown into the Abyss for a thousand years. We find in Revelation 20:4 that those who did not take the mark of the beast and were beheaded are resurrected and reign with Christ and the saints that were raptured. Revelation 20:7-10 explains the events at the end of the thousand-year reign.

Revelation 20:1-15 is the great white throne judgment, which ushers in the follower's eternal life with Christ in the New Jerusalem. Until the church, the followers of Christ, begin their wonderful eternal life with Christ in the new and perfect world, there is a great example of faith in Christian living found in Acts 6 and 7. Stephen, a dedicated follower of Christ, encourages others by his example of love, courage and faith in Christ.

Acts 6:8 describes Stephen as a man "full of God's grace and power". The verse also says that Stephen did "great wonders and miraculous signs among the people". (NIV) Like jealous and power hungry, religious leaders did to Christ, Acts 6:13 says that they seized Stephen and brought him to the Sanhedrin (their religious council). Also, like they did to Christ, they produced false witnesses. Acts 6:15 says they, "looked intently at Stephen, and they saw that his face was like the face of an angel". In Acts 7, Stephen shares a powerful testimony. After Stephen's great, spiritual testimony, Acts 7:54 (NIV) says, "they were furious and gnashed their teeth at him". But Stephen's response was spiritual, "Stephen, full of the Holy

Spirit, looks up to heaven and saw the glory of God, and Jesus standing at the right hand of God". In Acts 7:55 Stephen shared what he saw, and it was more than their carnal and secular minds could take. They covered their ears; took him outside the city and stoned him to death.

Some pagans as well as some believers might say in response to Stephen's exemplary faith, "I'm no Billy Graham or Mother Theresa". There is only one Billy Graham and one Mother Theresa, but there are millions more who have their own calling. We are not all great speakers or all great care givers, but every follower of Christ has a part in the church or body of Christ. The attitude of the religious leaders of the Sanhedrin in Jerusalem were not unlike the attitude that we see today in many pagans, including Hollywood liberals, cynical professors, hypocritical politicians, practitioners of pagan religions and many others who dislike the beliefs and ways of the followers of Christ.

The ways of the world won't last much longer. The unbelieving pagans will get their just reward. In Revelation 20:12, the book of life is opened. Revelation 20:15 (NIV) says, "If anyone's name was not found written in the book of life, he was thrown into the lake of fire". It's a shame that many teachers and preachers of organized religion today don't give people fair warning about sin, Satan, demons, the judgments of God, hell and the lake of fire. We all want to hear about love, and we need to practice more of God's love, but we are not doing people justice, if we don't share the truth of the whole gospel.

The good news is that the followers of Christ will be in the book of life! They are the ones not shaken by the coming apocalypse, and they are preparing for the rapture! The prophecy and vision of the Apostle John in Revelation 21:1 (NIV) says, "Then I saw a new heaven and a new earth, for the first heaven and the first earth had passed away". In verse 2,

John says that the Holy City is the new Jerusalem, which came from heaven. Verse 3 says that God will live with men! In Revelation 21:8 is a sober warning about sin.

In Revelation 21, John describes the greatness and beauty of the New Jerusalem. Its size in length, width and height and its beauty are phenomenal, but it can only best be described as the apostle describes it. Revelation 21:23 (NIV) says, "The city does not need the sun or the moon to shine on it, for the glory of God gives it light, and the Lamb is its lamp". Nations and kings will walk by the light, and nothing impure will enter the city. The only ones who enter the city will be, "those whose names are written in the Lamb's book life". Revelation 21:27

The beauty of Revelation 21 continues to the next chapter. In Revelation 22, the river of life is described. In verse 7, Jesus says, "Behold I am coming soon! Blessed is he who keeps the words of the prophecy in this book". Again in Revelation 22:12, the Apostle John quotes Christ, "Behold, I am coming soon! My reward is with me, and I will give to everyone according to what he has done". John begins to conclude Revelation and the Bible, when he says in verse 17, "The Spirit and the bride say, "Come!" And let him who hears say, "Come!" Whoever is thirsty let him come, and whoever wishes, let him take the free gift of the water of life".

There is a warning in the next chapter that all people who are part of manufactured religions, sects and cults should seriously think about. In Revelation 22:18, 19 (NIV), the prophet, the Apostle John, writes, "I warn everyone who hears the words of the prophecy of this book: If anyone adds anything to them, God will add to him the plagues described in this book. And if anyone takes words away from this book of prophecy, God will take away from him his share in the tree of life and in the holy city which are described in this book".

2 Timothy 4:3 warns us that many people will depart from the faith, and will listen to false teachers who satisfy their own carnal desires. Paul wrote the letter to Timothy to help him with instructions in the gospel. Paul prophesies that in the end time there will be false teachers who will mislead pagans and believers.

In Revelation 22 religions are condemned for not practicing the whole gospel. Some religions are centuries old, and some are newer. God's Word is not putting people down, but its intent is to lift them up and give them new life. Verse 20 quotes Christ again, "Yes, I am coming soon". In Revelation 22:21 (NIV), the Apostle John gives a blessing to the followers of Christ, "The grace of the Lord Jesus be with God's people. Amen".

Those who doubt can be prayed for. I ask the doubters and unbelievers to remember the characters in the cartoons holding the sign, "The End is Near!" The guy holding the sign is not the crazy one: the crazy ones are the ones who don't believe him! It is like the people of Noah's day who didn't believe Noah. The New Jerusalem that we read about at the end of Revelation is breathtaking. Who would want to miss out on all that God has in store for his faithful followers? Hebrews 10:37 gives us fair warning in preparing for the approaching apocalypse, "For in just a little while, He who is coming will come and will not delay".

I had the privilege of traveling from Indiana to Texas in the 1970s and working in evangelism before our American culture had changed. In those days many churches were interested in revival. Today many churches have their own spin on revival, and most churches don't have revival meetings. The United Methodist Church grew in the nineteenth century with revival meetings. I agree with Bob Farr of the Missouri Conference that we need more dedicated, followers of Christ rather than just more church members. The church needs to build disciples dedicated to outreach and revival.

Today we should be in prayer for teachers, nurses, pastors, police officers and other professionals because the powers of darkness are trying to work against them. My wife and I are bewildered about hospitals making nurses work twelve to fourteen hour shifts, when they become too tired to properly care for patients. Our society needs to be more considerate and respectful of professionals like nurses, pastors, teachers and police officers. If the hospital directors don't properly take care of their nurses, the nurses can't properly take care of the patients.

Most people leading protests stand for nothing and do little. If they were dedicated professionals, they would be helping our society instead of hurting it. It's easy to criticize and destroy (the broad way), but it's a challenge and takes hard work to improve the churches, schools and hospitals (the narrow way). Our prayer should be for people to take the narrow and strait way that leads to life, instead of the broad way that leads to destruction. Jesus told his followers, "You are the light of the world". (Matthew 5:14 NIV) It's up to the followers of Christ to show and tell the people of world that the truth is in Christ. Those who are "the light of the world" have little time to show others how to follow Christ and how to be prepared.

Great prophets like John, Peter and Paul, and Jesus himself have warned us to be prepared, because Christ is coming soon. As I prepared to do revival work in Oklahoma in late 1973 and 1974, there were recurrences of the same event along highways in Oklahoma and Texas. The federal government had passed a law that states needed to lower their speed limits from 70 mph to 55 mph on the interstate highways. In 1974, Texas and Oklahoma were two of the last states to lower their speed limit to 55 mph.

In 1973 there was a phenomenon in Texas and Oklahoma while their speed limits were still 70 mph. The very same event happened on a number of highways in the two states, but on one stretch of highway the same event happened the same way several times. The most dramatic time was when it happened to a reputable neuro surgeon. He said that he was driving along the highway, when he saw an elderly man hitchhiking. He said that he normally would not pick up a hitchhiker, but something drew him over to the shoulder, and he picked up the elderly man.

The elderly man got in the back seat. The doctor continued down the highway, and the man would repeat himself at times and say, "the Lord is coming real soon". The doctor hadn't said anything. In the 1970s models, there were no consoles, and the back of the seat went straight across to the passenger's side. The doctor finally stretched his arm across the seat to make a remark after the elderly man again said, "the Lord is coming real soon". When the doctor turned his head to make his reply, the old man had disappeared from the car while it was still going 70 mph!

The doctor was so shook up that he pulled off at the next exit into a gas station. At that time, the station still offered full service, and when the doctor got out and leaned up against the side of his car, the station attendant came over and asked, "what can I help you with?" The doctor was still trembling and was hesitant in speaking, and the attendant said, "you don't have to tell me: you just saw an angel, didn't you?" The attendant said that it had happened to several other motorists, who also pulled into his station.

Jesus warned and promised us that He is coming soon. The disciples told us that He is coming soon. Angels have told us that He is coming soon. What else will it take in the world for people to understand that He is coming soon? All that is left to be said is to be prepared. We are in the age and signs of the end time, and there are many undisputable signs. He is coming real soon. May the Lord be with you as you prepare for His coming.

www.ingramcontent.com/pod-product-compliance
Lightning Source LLC
Chambersburg PA
CBHW070603010526
44118CB00012B/1436